WAN
DER
ESS

WAND

THE UNEARTH WOMEN GUIDE TO TRAVELING SMART, SAFE, AND SOLO

ERESS

NIKKI VARGAS & ELISE FITZSIMMONS

with Brooke Saward, Oneika Raymond, Kelly Lewis,
Annika Ziehen, Dani Heinrich, and Esme Benjamin

Illustrations by Lucy Engelman

CLARKSON POTTER/
PUBLISHERS
NEW YORK

CONTENTS

INTRODUCTION

From traveling as a woman of color or a member of the LGBTQIA+ community to your first time solo traveling abroad or flying while pregnant, there is no one-size-fits-all style when it comes to women's travel. That's where we come in! This book is full of expert travel tips pulled from the experiences of Brooke Saward, Oneika Raymond, Kelly Lewis, Annika Ziehen, Dani Heinrich, Esme Benjamin, and us—Nikki Vargas and Elise Fitzsimmons.

Here you'll find inspiration for your next trip, tips that address the nuances of traveling as a woman today, a quiz to help you choose your next destination, packing checklists, and even a worksheet to help you build your very own Feminist City Guide.

You may be wondering who exactly we are and what the heck a Feminist City Guide is. Well, we are the founders of *Unearth Women*, a print and digital travel magazine dedicated to lifting women's voices, sharing travel stories, and pointing travelers in the direction of women- and BIPOC-owned businesses around the world. We like to say that our publication is a place where feminism meets travel. Of course, we have been asked what exactly that means, so here's how we think of it: While everyone has the ability to support feminism, we believe that travelers are uniquely positioned to both support women and spotlight their stories around the globe.

This is where our Feminist City Guides come in. Our guides encourage travelers to discover a destination through the lens of supporting its female entrepreneurs and honoring the women who have helped shape it. By the time you finish reading this book, you'll have your very own Feminist City Guide and you'll be able to navigate the world confidently.

With the help of our expert contributors, we will explore everything from staying safe abroad to navigating periods, pregnancy, and menopause during your adventures. And while this book is largely focused on the female travel experience, anyone with a passion for seeing the world will find invaluable information within these pages. Whether you're keen to volunteer at a sanctuary in Thailand or have discovered a newfound love for scuba diving, *Wanderess* has a little something for everyone.

Our hope is that this book becomes a beloved travel companion for you; that its pages will hold sand from far-flung beaches in Bali and pressed flowers from fields in Tuscany; and its margins will be full of scribbled notes and memories. Wherever your journey takes you, we want to help you travel better and smarter, and honor the impact women have on society—for truly, SHEroes can be found anywhere.

Show us where this book takes you by tagging your travel photos with #UnearthWomen on social media. And make sure to visit us at unearthwomen.com for more travel guides and information.

NIKKI VARGAS
Founding Editor and Cofounder,
Unearth Women

ELISE FITZSIMMONS
Publisher and Cofounder,
Unearth Women

DEFINE YOUR TRAVEL STYLE

WHAT IS YOUR

1. YOU ARE GIVEN MONEY TO PLAN ANY TRIP—WHERE DO YOU GO?

A) Iceland! I can't wait to lose myself in nature and the open road.

B) Anywhere with a beach, fruity cocktails, and sunny weather.

C) Somewhere I can make a difference and support the locals.

D) Sign me up for a wine tour of Tuscany, please.

E) A trip to Berlin where I can roam the streets on my own terms and discover hidden gems.

2. WHAT ARE YOUR IDEAL ACCOMMODATIONS?

A) Anything out of the ordinary: treehouse, yurt, or bungalow, I don't care—the more unconventional, the better.

B) A beachside resort with a spa. I'm ready for my massage!

C) A local homestay where I can really get to know the people.

D) A hotel within walking distance of restaurants and markets.

E) A hostel with communal areas where I can meet other travelers.

3. WHEN YOU ARRIVE AT YOUR DESTINATION, WHAT IS THE FIRST THING YOU DO?

A) Drop my bags off and go exploring. I don't like to waste a minute.

B) Meditate and unwind. I need time to get into vacation mode.

C) Look for volunteer opportunities I can sign up for while in town.

D) Go in search of my first meal, obviously.

E) Book a walking tour so I can get to know the city.

4. WHAT SETTING DO YOU PREFER WHEN YOU TRAVEL?

A) Mountains and wilderness.

B) A white-sand beach and clear waters.

C) An off-the-beaten-path village.

D) A local food market bursting with produce.

E) A European city where I can wander.

5. YOU HAVE A DAY TO YOURSELF— WHICH OF THE FOLLOWING ACTIVITIES DO YOU BOOK?

A) Sign me up for a zip-lining tour in the jungle.

B) An oceanfront yoga class.

TRAVEL STYLE?

C) A visit to a co-op of female artisans.

D) A cooking class with a local female chef.

E) I prefer to roam around the city and discover things myself.

6. WHICH SENTENCE BEST DESCRIBES YOU WHEN YOU TRAVEL?

A) I'm a thrill seeker looking for that next adrenaline rush.

B) I just want to relax and practice self-care.

C) I want to immerse myself in the community.

D) I love tasting new cuisines and getting to know a culture through its food.

E) I am independent and love to do my own thing.

7. WHEN IT COMES TO YOUR SOCIAL CIRCLE, YOU ARE THE ONE WHO ALWAYS:

A) Plans active outings like rock climbing or ice skating.

B) Enjoys catching up with friends over manicures.

C) Will suggest volunteering during the holiday season.

D) Loves to pick the restaurant.

E) Is comfortable taking yourself on a solo movie date.

8. WHEN YOU ARE AT HOME, HOW DO YOU RELAX?

A) A hike in the woods.

B) A massage or facial.

C) Volunteering at the local animal shelter.

D) Discovering a new restaurant.

E) Spending time alone with yourself.

9. WHICH OF THE FOLLOWING DESTINATIONS WOULD YOU BOOK A TRIP TO?

A) Norway

B) Costa Rica

C) Tanzania

D) Italy

E) New York City

10. WHAT IS YOUR DREAM TRIP?

A) Hiking in Patagonia.

B) Staying in an overwater bungalow in the Maldives.

C) Volunteering with elephants in Thailand.

D) Eating my way through the famed Basque country in northern Spain.

E) Backpacking solo throughout Southeast Asia.

YOU'RE AN
ADVENTURE
TRAVELER

Adventure starts where your comfort zone ends, and this can mean something very different for each of us. An adventure trip can mean hiking a mountain, going on safari, roaming the jungle in search of gorillas, taking a bike tour of Amsterdam, or exploring Vietnam by motorbike. You can find an adventure just about anywhere, but some countries prove more of a magnet for female adventure travelers.

ANNIKA ZIEHEN

My first adventure trip found me in Borneo where names like "Headhunters' Trail" and "Survivor Island" made me feel like an explorer. Before that, I never considered myself the adventuring type. I ended up in Sipadan, which is the only oceanic island in Malaysia and a place that makes scuba divers' hearts beat faster. On my first dive, I fearlessly rolled off the boat and found an exciting new home below the surface of the ocean. Ever since then, I have decided on my own definition of adventure. For me, I don't look for adventures on mountaintops or in jungles, but rather, ninety feet below the ocean's surface.

DESTINATIONS FOR ADVENTURE TRAVELERS

BORNEO

Borneo is the third-largest island in the world, shared by Malaysia, Indonesia, and Brunei. Most adventures in Borneo revolve around hiking and wildlife encounters, as the island is best known for its wild orangutan population. The best way to experience Borneo is by group tour, which allows safe access to some of the more off-the-beaten-path areas on the island, and female-run tours, many of which are exclusive to women. While Sabah and Sarawak are the most popular states for adventure travelers, if you want to see orangutans in the wild head to Tanjung Puting National Park on the Indonesian side of the island. Because Borneo is split by three countries, make sure to check visa requirements when traveling to different regions, as you might end up crossing borders.

ICELAND

This North Atlantic island is known as one of the safest travel destinations for women. For adventure travelers, Iceland boasts a full spectrum of activities—from chasing the Northern Lights to ice climbing the waterfalls outside of Reykjavík. For scuba divers, a special highlight awaits at Silfra in Thingvellir National Park. Here, you can dive into crystal-clear waters and snorkel in two continents at once as the tectonic plates of North America and Eurasia meet at Silfra.

SOUTH AFRICA

Simply put, South Africa was made for adventure travelers. Here, you can take a women-only safari through national parks and come face-to-face with wild lions, elephant herds, and some of the last rhinos on earth. If you want to get even closer to nature, go for a hike in the Drakensberg Mountains or hit the rock climber's paradise in Cederberg. For adrenaline junkies, you'll find the highest commercial bungee jump in the world at Bloukrans Bridge. For divers, the annual Sardine Run is one of the largest marine life migrations on earth.

"EVER FELT AFRAID OF EMBARKING ON A NEW ADVENTURE? THAT'S OKAY. FEAR IS NORMAL. WHAT'S IMPORTANT IS WHAT YOU DO WITH THE FEAR. BECAUSE, IN MY OPINION, FEAR IS JUST A SIGN THAT SOMETHING MATTERS IN YOUR LIFE— A SIGN THAT YOU'RE ABOUT TO STEP INTO SOMETHING MEANINGFUL."

RACHEL RUDWALL

MULTIMEDIA PRODUCER, HOST, EXPLORER, AND FOUNDER OF @RACHELROAMS

IF YOU ANSWERED MOSTLY

B

YOU'RE A

WELLNESS

TRAVELER

The appeal of a wellness-focused retreat is becoming more prominent given our busy schedules, constant online presence, and growing need to "switch off." Mental health is at the forefront of these retreats, often supplemented by relaxing activities and connecting with nature. If you're looking for an office escape or a chance to center yourself, these countries are ideal.

THAILAND

Thailand is a sanctuary for spiritual healing. Known for its tropical beaches, ancient ruins, and Buddhist beliefs, Thailand is a beacon for female wellness travelers looking to find purpose and power in themselves. Classic destinations such as Phuket and Koh Samui are now overrun by tourism, so be sure to look a little left of center when considering your location. Hua Hin in the south or Chiang Mai in the north are great places to start if you are looking for somewhere off the beaten path.

ZANZIBAR

When you think of wellness and relaxation retreats you might not immediately think of Zanzibar, the island paradise of East Africa. Zanzibar has much to offer by way of beautiful beaches, walks in the Jozani forest with red colobus monkeys, and seemingly endless days of sunshine. June through October is a great time of year to visit Zanzibar, when the temperatures and seasonal weather are more enjoyable.

BALI

Bali is an Indonesian island known for its scenic rice paddies, white-sand beaches, and beautiful culture. Bali and wellness retreats go hand in hand, but it isn't just yoga and smoothie bowls that you'll find here. Bali is a great destination for surf retreats, which are quickly becoming all the rage for first-time surfers looking to learn a new skill. However, if it *is* yoga you are after, head to the Ubud Yoga House. Founded by Sheila Burch back in 2014, this socially conscious yoga studio is nestled among rice paddies and offers daily classes. For yogis looking for teaching certification, you can join a program here that combines classes with accommodations.

INDIA

It could be said that India puts the "well" in "wellness." With spiritual depth, ancient rituals, and every type of yoga imaginable, India is a life-changing trip. Varanasi is considered the spiritual capital of India, where Hindus come to bathe in the sacred waters of the Ganges River. While here, take a river cruise down the Ganges to witness the nightly Arti Festival. In Jaipur, visit the Galtaji Temple where the freshwater springs are said to wash away sins. Near Mumbai, look to stay at Atmantan, a wellness resort offering the best range of therapies, from cocoon wraps to chakra cleansing—there is nothing this retreat won't cure through spiritual healing. Plan your trip to India between October and March, which is the best time to avoid monsoonal rains and to enjoy the warmth of the dry season. You can even visit India on a women-only tour, which will take you to numerous cities over the course of a few days.

COSTA RICA

If you're in need of finding the best version of yourself, look no further than Costa Rica. With rugged rainforests and a coastline bursting with biodiversity, this Central American country offers active wellness retreats for all travelers. From surfing to zip-lining through the jungle to relaxing in a cloud forest, Costa Rica has it all. Generally considered a safe destination for women to travel solo, it's recommended that you join a tour or travel as a group to more remote, rugged areas in the country. El Silencio Lodge & Spa sits on a private five-hundred-acre cloud forest reserve in Bajos del Toro, which has been declared a UNESCO heritage site. It is the perfect setting to connect with nature and rejuvenate oneself. December through April is the dry season and the ideal time to explore the rainforests, make use of the endless beaches, and book yourself for an active retreat.

YOU'RE A

VOLUNTEER

TRAVELER

Volunteering can be a wonderful way to get to know a culture, make some true and lasting friendships, and have a positive impact on local communities. Whether working with primates in Argentina or assisting single mothers in Thailand, volunteers have the power to create incredible change. If you're looking for a way to both see the world and give back, consider these programs.

NIKKI VARGAS

As an avid animal lover, my style of travel is one that finds me smiling in obscure dog shelters in Belize and seeking out ethical animal encounters at Thai elephant sanctuaries. I have been known to feed strays, volunteer at shelters, and befriend animals in almost every country I visit. I even adopted a dog while traveling in Central America! In a word, my style of travel is one focused on volunteer tourism with an emphasis on helping animals.

ARGENTINA

If you can pull yourself away from dancing the tango and drinking the wine, consider supporting the country's people and wildlife. Proyecto Carayá is a primate rehabilitation center that happens to be one of the few in the world that works with black howler monkeys. Volunteers who are passionate about animals and sustainability are invited to apply for their volunteer program, where accommodation and food are provided in exchange for a minimum fifteen-day commitment. If monkeys aren't your thing, the Food Bank Foundation is an opportunity to support Argentinian people facing hunger. Here, volunteers sort and classify donated food, check for expiration dates, make community visits, work on resource development, and help the food bank increase its distribution.

THAILAND

If you're headed to Thailand, volunteering at Elephant Nature Park in Chiang Mai is a must. Founded and operated by a local woman named Lek Chailert, Elephant Nature Park provides a sanctuary and rescue center for elephants, stray dogs, and cats. Lek's mission is to protect the Asian elephant through conservation and education. She founded the Save Elephant Foundation and is now running animal conservation projects in Cambodia and Myanmar in addition to Thailand. Elephant Nature Park is home to dozens of elephants and invites volunteers (both for day visits and long-term stays) to assist with feeding, bathing, walking, and working closely with the elephants and their handlers. Another organization worth volunteering for is Warm Heart Worldwide, a grassroots organization that empowers rural Thai villages through community-based initiatives focused on education, healthcare, and microenterprise.

MEXICO

Grupo Ecológico is the first environmental nonprofit focusing on the protection of sea turtles to be officially recognized by the Mexican government. The group aims to gather information and protect sea turtles, marine life, and the environment. Grupo Ecológico also has a mission to help improve the development of coastal communities through education, cleanup campaigns, and public health programs. Another volunteer organization worth exploring is Oaxaca-based SiKanda, which works toward creating a more just world with social and economic programs aimed at eradicating poverty and improving living conditions in Mexico.

SOUTH AFRICA

Gap Africa Projects offers programs in both conservation and education, which have been vetted to ensure they are having a truly positive impact. Similarly, Calabash Trust has been running philanthropic volunteer opportunities since 1999 and focuses on skill and knowledge exchanges that meet specific needs in local communities. Notably, Calabash Trust gets approval from the community before saying yes to a volunteer. For travelers looking to support South African wildlife, the South African Animal Sanctuary Alliance (SAASA) has three award-winning sanctuaries with ongoing volunteer positions.

YOU'RE A

FOODIE

TRAVELER

Culinary travel is often at the forefront of why we explore foreign lands. There is perhaps no better way to truly connect with a culture than through its food, passed down at the hands of locals for generations. Sure, you can find Italian food around the corner, but no matter how many pizzerias you frequent, they won't compare to an authentic Neapolitan pizza. If you travel for your taste buds, these destinations combine the best of flavor and culture.

ALSACE

With its unique position bordering France, Switzerland, and Germany, the Alsace region blends many typical French delicacies with a strong German influence. Here you can expect to find hearty and rich delicacies, such as pork sausages with sauerkraut and Tarte Flambée (aka Flammekeuche, or dough covered with crème fraîche and topped with onions, cheese, and bacon). If you're a wine drinker, Alsace is known for its white wines, particularly its dry Rieslings and Pinot Gris. For beer drinkers, Alsace both grows the hops and brews for the majority of the beer served in France.

BURGUNDY

Located in the center of France, Burgundy is one of the most famous wine regions in the world. Due to its ideal geography, climate, and soil, the Burgundy region is renowned for its Chardonnay, Pinot Noir, and Gamay grapes. In the Burgundy town of Chablis, just two hours from Paris, there has been a rise in female wine-makers worth visiting and supporting. Of course, with great wine comes great food. Expect to find incredible Michelin-starred restaurants throughout the region.

LYON

You will be forgiven for thinking Paris is the foodie capital of France when it is, in fact, Lyon. Dubbed the "World Capital of Gastronomy" back in 1935, Lyon is home to incredible chefs, the famed Les Halles de Lyon indoor market, and some true Lyonnaise specialties. There is no shortage of incredible restaurants of every caliber here, from street eats to multicourse fine dining experiences. The typical style of cuisine in Lyon is hearty and homey, with lots of cream, butter, and duck fat.

NAPLES

Naples is the third-largest city in Italy and the regional capital of Campania, but it is best known as the birthplace of pizza. Before pizza became what it is today, it was flatbread without the tomatoes. Then, in the 1700s, Naples upped the game by adding tomatoes and cheese atop the dough. Until you have pulled apart cheesy, tomato-covered slices in the streets of Naples, you can't really say you've tried pizza at all. There is nothing as comparably fresh to a true Neapolitan pizza, which is a thin-crust pie topped with fresh mozzarella, San Marzano tomatoes, and basil.

LOMBARDY

There's something incredibly special about rice that practically melts in your mouth. The technical term for this is risotto and the place to get it is Milan, the capital of Lombardy and the fashion, design, and commerce capital of Italy. It's here that you'll find the Trattoria Masuelli San Marco, where they have been cooking the traditional risotto alla Milanese recipe (made with saffron, onions, shallots, white wine, and Parmesan cheese) since their opening in 1921.

ROME

Rome is a place that combines ancient ruins with ancient recipes. Rome is the capital of both Italy and the Lazio region, known for its history and cuisine. While every dish is worth sampling, the simple-yet-spectacular spaghetti alla carbonara is one that can't be missed. This old dish is rumored to have once sustained Italy's charcoal workers, with the name *carbonara* deriving from the Italian word *carbonaro*, meaning "charcoal workers." Spaghetti alla carbonara is made with just five ingredients: pasta, guanciale, eggs, pecorino Romano cheese, and black pepper.

SICILY

Found just off the "toe" of Italy's boot, Sicily is the largest island in the Mediterranean Sea. Alongside pristine beaches and ancient architecture, Sicily's main draw is its food. While anything from arancini (deep-fried risotto balls) to pasta alla Norma is worth trying, it's the cannoli that steals the show. Cannoli can be found around the world, but nowhere is it crispier and creamier than in Sicily, its birthplace. Any pastry shop here will have an abundance of cannoli flavors and combinations on offer, though if you can find somewhere that fills shells to order, you will be guaranteed a cannoli experience you won't soon forget.

MEXICO

The flavors of Mexico have long been favorites around the world; however, there is nowhere better to try Mexican cuisine than in Mexico itself. The two destinations to visit when heading to Mexico on a culinary adventure are Mexico City and Oaxaca. Mexico City has quickly become a foodie hotspot, perhaps known best for their tacos al pastor. These slowly spit-roasted pork tacos were originally brought to Mexico by Lebanese immigrants, and are now found around the city in street carts and markets. Less than six hours away is Oaxaca, a colorful city known for its seven different types of moles. These thick, slow-cooked sauces add flavor to just about everything in Oaxaca, but when given the option to choose, go for the mole negro, which has a savory-sweet taste.

MOROCCO

Morocco is a vibrant North African country bordering the Atlantic Ocean and the Mediterranean Sea, and is home to colorful architecture, epic scenery, and aromatic spices sold in ancient souks. You'll find some of the best food in the capital city of Marrakech. One of the most popular dishes to order in Morocco is tajine. *Tajine* refers to both the name of the dish and the clay pot with a cone-shaped lid in which a medley of vegetables and meat are slow-cooked for hours. Wash down the tajine with some traditional Moroccan mint tea, which is sold on nearly every corner and made with fresh mint.

JAPAN

It comes as no surprise that Japan is a destination for seafood lovers. In the land of sushi and sashimi, you will find some of the freshest seafood on earth. Most Japan-bound travelers start their journey in Tokyo, the capital of the country. While you're bound to find quality sushi almost anywhere in Tokyo, those in search of the best will head to the Tsukiji Market. The "inner market" of Tsukiji was once a tourist draw for its famous tuna auctions, but in 2018 they moved to Toyosu. You may not find the tuna auction and wholesale market in Tokyo's Tsukiji Market today, but you will find a slew of restaurants and shops serving fresh sushi and sashimi. If you're looking to eat sushi *and* to support women, head to Nadeshiko Sushi, which is Japan's first all-female sushi restaurant. Another popular dish to try in Japan is, of course, the ramen. In a city that is home to the most Michelin-starred restaurants in the world, ramen offers a delicious and affordable option for budget travelers.

YOU'RE A
SOLO
TRAVELER

Solo travel can be many things: an introspective journey, a chance to travel on your own terms, an opportunity to make friends in new places. Whether writing in your journal at a Parisian café or befriending bunkmates in a Buenos Aires hostel, solo travel forces you to step beyond your comfort zone and tap into your inner confidence. On such soul-searching journeys, certain destinations are more conducive to solo travelers in terms of safety and connecting with other globetrotters.

BROOKE SAWARD

Back when I started exploring the world alone, travel was more expensive and much more of a luxury than it is today. I was studying and working full-time to save for my first big trip: traveling solo for a year after I finished college. On graduation day, I booked a one-way ticket to London and began a journey that would take me across Europe, South America, North America, Asia, Oceania, and the Middle East for twelve months. That was more than eight years ago and I've been on the move ever since.

DESTINATIONS FOR SOLO TRAVELERS

SPAIN

Spain has become one of the first countries to introduce a women-only hotel. It should come as no surprise then that this Western European gem is considered a top destination for solo female travelers today. From the beautiful Mediterranean coastline to exciting cities like Madrid, you'll find culinary delights with ample opportunities to connect with fellow wayfarers.

Barcelona, the capital city of Catalonia, is a great city to visit for a first-time solo traveler. Delight in culinary gems at the famed La Boqueria market or bask in the artistic genius of Gaudi at Park Güell—this vibrant city has a little something for everyone. If it's your first time visiting, book a hotel near Las Ramblas, Barcelona's main pedestrian-only street. Considered the center of the city, there is always something to enjoy on Las Ramblas—from street performances to street food. Las Ramblas is also right near La Boqueria, which is best enjoyed in the early morning hours.

COLOMBIA

The idea of solo traveling as a woman in Colombia may raise a few eyebrows, but when it comes to the seaside city of Cartagena, this Caribbean destination could not be safer or more accommodating. From Miami-like Bocagrande to the artistic Getsemani, Cartagena's neighborhoods each carry a distinct personality. Cartagena's Old City is like stepping into the romantic pages of a Gabriel García Márquez novel. Cobblestone streets wind their way beneath brightly colored balconies dripping with tropical flowers. Street vendors sell handmade arepas and fresh tropical fruit, while travelers relax at outdoor cafés with a cold cerveza in hand. Day trips to the nearby Islas del Rosario offer solo travelers a chance to swap the Old City for the pristine sandy beaches of Playa Blanca for a few hours. Or, for a more offbeat day trip, solo travelers can venture to the nearby Volcán del Totumo, a mystical mud-filled volcano said to be infused with healing properties. In street-art-splashed Getsemani, popular hostels—Media Luna and Mamallena—offer an array of weekly parties. The two hostels are a great place to meet other solo travelers, enjoy cheap festivities, and save on booking affordable day trips. If hostels are not your thing, stay at one of the many hotels in the Old City and enjoy mojitos in the shadow of the famed Botero sculpture in Plaza Santo Domingo.

ICELAND

While Iceland is a prime destination for adventure lovers, it also happens to be one of the best destinations for solo female travelers. Fly into Keflavik and make your way to Iceland's capital, Reykjavík—the country's largest city. A mere forty-five minutes from the famed Blue Lagoon, you can begin your solo adventure with a relaxing visit to the mineral-rich waters of the world-famous hot springs. Once settled in Reykjavík, you'll find the capital to be a small and walkable city boasting a variety of restaurants, shops, and cozy hotels to choose from. For solo female travelers who are not renting a car, Reykjavík is a great place to stay and book day trips out of. The city is driving distance from many of the Golden Circle's main attractions, allowing easy access to the country's natural beauty from the convenience and safety of a guided tour. After day trips spent exploring geysers, waterfalls, and lava fields, make sure to check out activities closer to the city center, like whale watching, trying a classic Icelandic hot dog, or visiting the Penis Museum (yes, this really exists).

GETTING READY FOR YOUR NEXT TRIP

RESEARCHING A DESTINATION before a trip can benefit you in many ways. For starters, you can save yourself headaches by having a basic understanding of your destination—from the best neighborhoods to stay in to the easiest ways to get around, research will help you organize your trip well ahead of time. But beyond building a restaurant wish list, getting to know your destination in advance can help maximize your travel time, point you in the right direction (literally), and help you discover hidden gems along the way. One of the more important reasons to do your research is to arrive in a country with an understanding of the current social and political situation. This can help travelers better navigate cultural sensitivities, have more meaningful connections with locals, and learn how to support the community.

WHAT TO KNOW
BEFORE YOU GO

You've booked your flight, chosen your hotel, and have officially entered that blissful pre-trip period. Now it's time to check out...

LOCAL NEWS AND SOCIAL MEDIA

Local news is a great resource to learn about what's happening in a country from a social, cultural, and political standpoint. This is especially important to know ahead of time if you are visiting a country that is experiencing political turmoil, riots, or other tumultuous events, so you can be prepared upon arrival. A simple web search will often bring a wealth of information about your destination. For broadscale social and political information, check out centrist news sources like Al Jazeera and BBC World before and during your travels. Social media is also a great resource where you can find real-time information on everything from new restaurant openings to water quality updates. Search for expat communities who live in your destination and check relevant hashtags for up-to-date information.

ONLINE TRAVEL GROUPS FOR WOMEN

There are a plethora of women's travel groups to keep you connected while abroad. On social media, groups like Women Who Travel and Girls LOVE Travel tap a network of more than one million ladies all eager to offer advice about anything from the best ice cream shops to a country's dating culture. Outside of social media, members-only groups like Wanderful and El Camino Travel help foster a sense of community through workshops, in-person meetups, homestays, and on-the-ground information. If you are headed on a trip, these social groups provide the perfect forum to ask destination-specific advice and

NIKKI VARGAS

In my early twenties, I arrived in Uruguay without so much as an idea of what the local currency was. I had taken a spontaneous ferry ride from nearby Buenos Aires where I had been solo traveling. As I boarded the ferry, I realized I was not prepared to visit Colonia whatsoever. Looking back, my limited time in Uruguay was marked by wandering aimlessly and not learning a thing about the country I was in. Flash forward to my thirties: I now arrive in a country carrying a guidebook bursting with handwritten notes and local phrases. I have come to value the art of preparing for a trip and appreciating a country's culture before my plane's wheels hit the tarmac.

connect with local women. Mobile networking apps (also see resources) are also a fun and convenient way to meet fellow female travelers.

LOCAL LITERATURE BY WOMEN

Chances are there are plenty of great books about your destination written by prominent local authors. A quick online search will reveal the must-read books for the country you are visiting, which is a great way to grow appreciation for the destination and learn about its history. To better understand the country through the eyes of women, search for books by local female authors. These books are a good way to both support female authors and understand the female experience in a foreign country.

DOCUMENTARIES, VLOGS, AND BLOGS

These days, streaming services are bursting with documentaries that provide powerful and insightful views into countries and cultures all over the world. Look for documentaries about the destination you are visiting to get a feel for its history and culture. Similarly, vlogs and blogs can show you what it's like to actually travel in your destination country. Many travelers take joy in documenting their trips and sharing their journey on personal blogs or sites like YouTube or Vimeo. These firsthand accounts of a traveler's experiences are an excellent resource for where to eat, what neighborhoods to stay in, nearby day trips to take, and practical information.

COOKING CLASSES AND HOSTED DINNERS

Ahead of arriving at your destination, book experiences that can introduce you to a destination's culture and people. Companies like EatWith offer dinners or cooking classes at a vetted host's home. Similarly, Airbnb Experiences offers a variety of unique classes, walking tours, and dinners (many of which are hosted by women) to better acquaint travelers with locals. When participating in community and home-cooked meals, you are nearly guaranteed to experience something special. For example, a homestay in Mongolia could introduce you to homemade yak yogurt cake, a dish you'll dream of for years to come.

PRACTICE THE LANGUAGE FIRST

Learning the language before you go offers a leg up for any adventurer. While taking a continuing education class for a one-week trip might not be realistic, interactive language apps like Duolingo allow you to practice basic phrases ahead of your vacation. A good old-fashioned pocket dictionary is also a solid choice for looking up and jotting down phrases you hear often or want to remember. Prior to arrival, download a translate app to your smartphone. Many apps can listen to a speaker and spit out a translation, making conversation much easier. Download the local language and save some of the key phrases that you may need in a pinch.

TRAVEL
HACKING 101

Travel hacking is a nifty set of tools that helps travelers find savvy ways to shave dollars off their trips. Often the art of travel hacking revolves around using a travel credit card that earns you miles and points with every purchase, which can be redeemed for low-cost flights. But what if you don't have a travel credit card? The good news is that you can still use some of these hacks.

HOW TO
SAVE ON AIRFARE

BE FLEXIBLE WITH TIMING

The cheapest days to fly, inbound and outbound, are Tuesdays and Wednesdays, while Sundays are the most expensive. On average, flying midweek is nearly $85 USD cheaper than flying on a Sunday. Similarly, flying at inconvenient times—such as early-morning "red-eye" flights or late-night departures—will invariably save you money.

FLYING INTO AN ALTERNATIVE AIRPORT

If traveling to a destination with multiple airports, explore the difference in pricing for landing in an alternate airport. For example, landing in Newark Liberty when visiting New York City will almost always offer lower airfare than landing at LaGuardia or JFK. This trick also works for regional and rural airports when you are planning on renting a car. If you are planning a trip to the High Rockies of Colorado, consider flying into Colorado Springs Airport over Denver International Airport. The drive time is similar and you will save money on both the flight and the rental car.

KNOWING WHEN TO BOOK

There are many schools of thought about the best time to book a flight. However, a good rule of thumb is fifty days out from your travel date. To take the guesswork out of when to book, there are mobile apps that take on the task of monitoring flight prices and alerting you to the best time to book. We recommend watching flights with the app Hopper. Hopper monitors fluctuations in airfare for a particular route and will predict whether the current flight prices will rise or fall in the weeks leading up to your trip. All you have to do is sit back and wait for Hopper to give you the green light to book your flight. Similarly, sites like Skiplagged show you the historic pricing, so you can see in real time whether you are getting a good deal. If your flight is ready to book but you're waiting on your next paycheck, services like Airfordable allow you to pay for airfare in monthly installments.

CLEAR YOUR COOKIES AND GO INCOGNITO

Most airline sites monitor user visitation and serve higher flight prices based on their flight searches. If you have been keeping an eye on that round-trip flight to Paris, your browser cookies will let the flight-search site know and you'll often be shown a higher price the next time you visit the site. Clear your browser cookies and open an incognito page to make sure you're truly seeing the best flight deals.

THE MAGIC OF THIRD-PARTY SEARCH ENGINES

Third-party sites are a great way to navigate your way to the least expensive flights out there. Search engines like Momondo, Skyscanner, or Hipmunk share lower airfares with more itinerary options to choose from. Most sites will automatically mix and match for the best fare options. However, because it is an algorithm, it's always worth comparing the third-party results with the prices available on the airline's direct booking site. Subscribe to email lists like Scott's Cheap Flights, which provide regular information on limited-time flight deals. One more thing to remember: When using these sites, remember the fares are minimal and usually don't include baggage fees, priority boarding, or even meals.

USING THE "HIDDEN CITIES" TRICK

The "hidden cities" trick helps travelers save on airfare by focusing on flight itineraries with layovers. For example, let's say you're looking for affordable flights to Reykjavík. With the "hidden city" trick, you may purchase a cheaper flight to London with a layover in Iceland. You would simply board in New York, deplane in Iceland, and skip your connection to London. For those willing to travel with carry-on only luggage, this trick can save you more money than booking a direct flight to your destination.

BOOK "IN-COUNTRY" RATES

When booking a flight directly through an international airline, pull up the site in the native language, in the incognito browser, to save some serious money. Often flights are more expensive for international customers, so a way to side-step being charged extra is to view the airline site in the local language or by using a VPN to set your IP address to that specific country.

A CHECKLIST FOR AFFORDABLE AIRFARE

O   Sign up for a travel rewards credit card.

O   Subscribe to a flight deals newsletter, such as Airfare Watchdog.

O   Choose your trip dates (remember that Tuesdays and Wednesdays are the best days for cheaper travel).

O   Download an app like Hopper and input your travel dates to see the best time to book your flight.

O   Before you book a flight, clear your browser cookies and open an incognito browser page.

O   Use third-party airfare sites like Momondo and Skyscanner (remember to compare prices to flights sold directly by airlines to make sure you're getting the best possible deal).

O   Consider using the "hidden city" trick or add an extra destination to your trip by booking a layover.

O   If you can't afford to book your flight just yet, use Airfordable of Affirm.

CONSIDER CONNECTING FLIGHTS

While the "hidden cities" travel hack will have you skipping your connecting flight altogether, another way to save money and add a destination to your itinerary is through flight connections. For example, booking a direct flight from Dallas to Paris will be more costly than booking a connecting flight from Dallas to New York and then onward to Paris. If you have the time, a connecting flight not only saves you money but can give you a fun layover in an exciting city. Depending on the city you layover in, a few hours may be all that you need to get a taste of it. Most airfare search engines allow you to filter results by length of trip, which is perfect for choosing longer layovers. If you want to enjoy your layover sans carry-on bags, use apps like Stasher to find hotels and stores that will securely store your bag for a fee.

HOW TO
PACK LIKE A PRO

Unless you plan to hit your next destination with only the clothes on your back or go on a shopping spree, packing is the most essential part of traveling. These tried-and-true packing tricks will help you tackle your suitcase with ease.

EXPERT
PACKING TIPS

CREATE A STANDARD PACKING LIST

Packing becomes less annoying and a lot more efficient when you have a clear idea of what you'll actually need to bring. Create a master packing checklist, then tailor it for each trip. If boarding a long-haul flight, always be sure to include a spare toiletry bag in your carry-on. When you're on hour fifteen of a seventeen-hour flight to Hong Kong, you'll be grateful you thought to pack a toothbrush and travel-size face wash.

PICKING THE RIGHT BAG

First, consider how you'll be traveling. Wheeled bags are easier on your back, but mean you'll have one less free hand to use. Will there be stairs or narrow train platforms that will make hefting large luggage impossible? Do you have a connecting flight that would make checking a bag riskier? Ensure that you can

ONIEKA RAYMOND

When I say I'm on the road a lot, I mean it. I visit around twenty countries and upward of forty cities each year. While often tiring, I can't deny the thrill of travel: the sights, sounds, new foods, and unexpected encounters. However, the one thing that I absolutely despise about traveling is packing. Despite this, my frequent travels have helped shape me into something of a packing pro.

manage the bag safely and quickly if you will be on your own. Test your bag and its weight out by wheeling or walking with it fully loaded around your house or block. Look for a bag that allows you to attach little locks.

CHECK YOUR AIRLINE'S BAGGAGE POLICY

There's nothing worse than getting to the airport and realizing that your luggage is over the weight limit, your carry-on is too large for the overhead bin, or they count your tiny purse as a carry-on. Check your airline's baggage policy in advance and pack your day purse into your carry-on to avoid extra baggage fees. In some smaller airports, the baggage fee can only be paid outside of the secure boarding area, which could result in a missed flight. For international flights, all passengers are required to check in at the kiosk; as a result all bags, even carry-ons, are subject to weight inspection.

HOW TO TRAVEL
WITH ONE BAG

From avoiding checked baggage fees to skipping the wait time at the baggage carousel, the benefits of going carry-on-only are endless—all you have to do is pack effectively, efficiently, and creatively.

PACK ONLY ONE WEEK OF CLOTHING

This is the cardinal rule of traveling with carry-on luggage only. Whether your trip is for a week or a month, pack no more than a week's worth of clothes, with the exception of underwear. Re-wear clothing, mix and match outfits, and refresh outfits with travel-size fabric freshener. If traveling long term, look for affordable laundry options at your destination. While most hotels will offer laundry services, you can save by washing your clothes at a local laundromat.

LEAVE THE HEAVY STUFF AT HOME

Clunky jewelry, weighty electronics, full-size toiletries—do you really need to take them with you? Get creative and substitute heavy items with lightweight accessories like scarves, a smartphone camera over a massive DSLR, and multiuse products such as 2-in-1 shampoo and conditioner. If you must bring a heavy sweater, jacket, or shoes with you, wear them on the plane so as not to take up space in your carry-on.

PACK ITEMS THAT CAN BE USED IN MULTIPLE WAYS

Scarves can be draped around the shoulders or neck, double as a head-wrap or covering, be used as a picnic blanket, or worn as a sarong. Liquid castile soap can be used for everything from washing your body to cleaning your clothes. C.O. Bigelow's Rose Salve can be used as both a lip balm and a salve for dry patches on your body and face. A small bottle of coconut oil can go a long way in acting as a hair defrizzer, makeup remover, face moisturizer, natural deodorant, and treatment for minor skin irritations. Your hair conditioner can double as shaving cream in a pinch. And a pillowcase can double as a laundry bag. The more items you can pack that serve more than one purpose, the less you'll need to carry.

CHOOSE A COLOR SCHEME

Packing complementary colors will result in more outfit options with fewer actual articles of clothing.

PRO TIP

Yellow, green, and orange palettes pop in photos.

PACK LESS MAKEUP

Instead of bringing your whole makeup bag, think about sticking to a few items that won't take up space but will pack a lot of punch. For example, mascara and a bold lipstick will elevate your look with minimal effort. Consider snagging samples of your favorite brands in lieu of full-size containers.

RESTRICT YOURSELF TO THREE PAIRS OF SHOES

Shoes are clunky and add lots of weight to luggage. Stick to three pairs of shoes: good walking shoes, a pair of shoes for going out, and a casual pair of shoes such as flip-flops or flats. Wear your bulkiest pair on the plane to save room in your bag.

ROLL THOSE CLOTHES

When going carry-on only, it's crucial to maximize space. One way to do this is by rolling your clothes rather than folding them. Rolling your pants, T-shirts, and socks helps minimize the amount of room they take up in your carry-on bag. Another great option is to use packing cubes (available online), which compress your clothing even further.

"I'M A STRONG BELIEVER IN 'LESS IS MORE.' THE LESS YOU TRAVEL WITH, THE MORE CONVENIENT IT WILL BE FOR YOU TO MOVE AROUND. LUGGING AROUND LOTS OF LUGGAGE WILL ONLY LEAD TO FRUSTRATION."

NELLIE HUANG

TRAVEL WRITER
AND PUBLISHED AUTHOR

TRANSPORTATION
ESSENTIALS

What is considered an essential item varies from traveler to traveler. Some put an emphasis on packing items that alleviate travel anxiety, while others search for maximum entertainment. Whatever your style, there are a few flight essentials every traveler should bring onboard.

COMPRESSION SOCKS

The benefits of compression socks include boosting blood circulation, minimizing leg swelling, and preventing the risk of blood clots.

WATER BOTTLE AND MOISTURIZERS

An aircraft's filtration system pulls outside air in and circulates it around the cabin, causing in-cabin humidity to drop to between 10 and 20 percent (between 30 and 60 percent is considered a comfortable humidity level for humans). Combat chapped skin and lips with a water bottle, face moisturizer, eye drops, and/or lip balm.

VITAMIN C PACKETS

An estimated one in every five passengers will catch a cold while flying. To help boost your immune system, consider bringing vitamin C packets to ward off illness.

ANTIBACTERIAL WIPES

Thousands of people fly each day and hundreds have sat in your very seat.

NIKKI VARGAS

For me, my travel essentials can be found in my "stress-free kit" (as I like to call it), which comes complete with lavender oil, finger fidgeters, CBD tablets, ginger chews, and chamomile tea packets to help me find serenity even at thirty-five thousand feet in the air.

Wipe away the germs with travel packs of antibacterial wipes and bring some hand sanitizer.

APPS FOR MEDITATION

If you're a nervous flier, a meditation app could help calm your anxiety. Apps like Headspace and Calm offer an array of audio programs to help you meditate and find restful sleep. Download your programs in advance so they are available for listening offline.

GINGER CHEWS

Ginger is proven to help calm upset stomachs and offset nausea, and it won't leave you drowsy—unlike over-the-counter anti-nausea medications.

HEADPHONES

While many airplanes offer complimentary headsets to passengers, it's always a good idea to bring your own headphones. Bonus if they're noise-canceling.

PORTABLE BATTERY

Bring a portable power battery just in case you find yourself on an older aircraft without charging outlets with hours of flying time ahead of you. They are also perfect for when you land at your destination and do not have time to charge your phone before hopping on transportation to your accommodations. Similarly, tossing one in your bag can prove to be a lifesaver when out and about for your day.

SNACKS

Many airlines only offer food for purchase these days. Rather than paying for expensive snacks onboard, bring some with you, such as granola bars or dried fruit. A cheese plate with fruit on the side is an excellent option. You're allowed to bring solid foods in your carry-on so long as they are sealed.

TRAVEL PILLOW, EYE MASK, AND EARPLUGS

If you're flying coach, this holy trinity is necessary to ensure a comfortable sleep. You can order cheap travel pillows online or purchase one last-minute at the airport.

"IF YOU MISS SOMETHING YOU NEED, YOU CAN ALWAYS BUY IT AT YOUR DESTINATION. IT MIGHT BE TRICKIER WHEN TRAVELING IN A DEVELOPING COUNTRY, BUT I'VE NEVER HAD ANY PROBLEMS FINDING BASIC NECESSITIES."

NELLIE HUANG

TRAVEL WRITER
AND PUBLISHED AUTHOR

BEFORE YOU
BOARD THE PLANE

GET IMMUNIZATIONS

If traveling internationally, check with the CDC well ahead of your trip to see if there are any routine, required, or recommended immunizations you might need or any entry/exit requirements for specific diseases.

SET UP TRAVEL ALERTS WITH YOUR BANK

Call your bank while you have reliable phone service. Tell them the places you plan on going, even if it is just for one night so you can avoid running into card issues abroad.

PRINT COPIES OF YOUR RESERVATIONS

In the event that your phone battery dies or you find yourself in a place that you'd rather not pull out a smartphone, have printed copies of your hotel reservations on hand.

PRINT COLOR COPIES OF YOUR PASSPORT

Keep printed copies of your passport in case your original goes missing or is stolen.

CONFIRM FLIGHT TRANSFERS

Double-check to see that your flight transfer is in the same airport. If it is not in the same airport, make sure that you have ample time to get to the other side of the city to catch your connecting flight.

CONNECT WITH LOCAL WOMEN AHEAD OF TIME

Ask your friends and family if they have any contacts in the country you are visiting. Likewise, online women's travel groups (see resources) are great for connecting with other women around the globe.

DOWNLOAD OFFLINE MAPS

Before you leave home, download local maps of your destination so you will be able to orient yourself without using data upon arrival. This is also a great option for road trips and cities where having a downloaded map coupled with your phone's location will make navigating far easier.

SHARE YOUR LOCATION

If traveling alone, let loved ones know where you are by updating your smartphone settings and sharing your location. Even when you are off Wi-Fi and data, your phone's position will update. This is especially important if you are planning to venture off-the-grid.

CHECK WATER QUALITY

Make sure you can drink the tap water in the country you are visiting. If the water is not potable, cut down on plastic bottles by bringing your own water bottle and using a UV filter to kill any pesky germs. Another option is iodine or Potable Aqua tablets to purify your water.

EXERCISE BEFORE AND AFTER YOUR FLIGHT

Light stretching and mild bodyweight exercises that focus on hip and spine mobility, like yoga, are a great preflight option. Using resistance bands or taking a run after your flight will help loosen up your limbs and get your blood moving.

FILL UP YOUR WATER BOTTLE

Once you are through security, fill up your bottle so that you can hydrate without waiting on the flight attendants to begin their service.

PACK A FIRST AID KIT

Speak to your doctor about how to put together a decent first aid kit. While ibuprofen and basic antibiotics are available in many parts of the world, a personalized first aid kit is especially important if you take any necessary medication or have certain allergies. Make sure to also carry a doctor's note if you have any special conditions.

PRE-FLIGHT CHECKLIST

○ Double-check your flight's baggage allowance.

○ Pack anything of value in your carry-on bag, including computers, cameras, and tablets.

○ Pack any essential medications in your carry-on.

○ Include compression socks in your carry-on bag for long-haul flights.

○ Bring a water bottle, lip balm, and moisturizer.

○ Bring a shawl or scarf for chilly flights.

○ Print physical copies of your hotel reservations, bookings, and passport.

○ Confirm flight transfers.

"CHOOSE SOMEWH
GOING TO BE COM
THERE'S GOING TO
OF FAMILIAR REF
WHEN YOU'RE CO
YOU'RE CONFIDE
CONFIDENT, YOU
VULNERABLE."

JESSICA NABONGO

TRAVEL WRITER AND TRAVEL EXPERT

ERE YOU'RE
FORTABLE, WHERE
BE SOME KIND
ERENCE POINT.
MFORTABLE,
NT. WHEN YOU'RE
WON'T BE AS

SAFE
AND
SANE

STAYING SAFE
WHILE TRAVELING

Whether the situation stems from parents, partners, or well-meaning strangers, female travelers are often confronted with questions of safety. Concerns about crime, health hazards, natural disasters, and even terrorism are risks that can pop up close to home as well as abroad. While some issues are beyond our control—and more about fear management than prevention—there are steps women can take to travel safely.

CHECK TRAVEL ADVISORIES

Look up travel advisories on the US Department of State's website. Most countries are ranked on four travel advisory levels, which range from "exercise normal precautions" to "do not travel." Many travel insurances will not cover you in countries with increased risk, so check countries you are visiting before purchasing coverage (see page 122). You'll also want to check whether the country maintains diplomatic or consular relations with your country. In some "high-risk" countries, an embassy will not be able to help you in an emergency. Should you decide to travel to a "high-risk" destination, enroll in the State Department's Smart Traveler Enrollment Program (STEP) before your trip.

ANNIKA ZIEHEN

I think nothing beats the ease and convenience of paying by credit card when I travel. I usually travel only with credit cards, and use them for both paying vendors and withdrawing money from an ATM. Except for very few countries where ATMs are sparse, this has always worked out well for me. While exchanging money is always an option, I like to travel with as little cash as possible.

KEEPING YOUR MONEY SAFE

Sure, credit and debit cards are convenient for traveling, but what do you do if your card is lost, stolen, or skimmed? Here are some steps you can take to protect your ATM and credit cards on your next trip.

- Inform your bank that you will be traveling overseas. This is especially important if you are planning to use your debit card to withdraw cash or make purchases.

- In case of a credit card being lost or stolen, have more than one credit card with you. Keep your backup credit card tucked away in your suitcase in case your wallet is stolen.

- Sign up for online banking and/or download your bank's mobile app to check your account regularly while traveling. If you have an iPhone, enable facial recognition, or set a passcode on your smartphone so that only you can access your mobile banking app.

- If you need to call your bank from overseas, use Skype's mobile app to avoid international charges.

- Change your online banking password prior to traveling and again upon your return home, just in case.

- Place a withdrawal limit on your card before your trip. That way if your ATM card is stolen or misplaced, your entire bank balance is protected.

- Use the ATMs inside of banks instead of on the street, and always protect your PIN.

- If caught without money, have family or friends send funds via PayPal, Venmo, Western Union, or Xoom.

MONEY AND VALUABLES

Keeping money and valuables secure can be an anxiety-inducing prospect, but with these tips, you can spend more time worrying about what sight to see next and less time checking on your valuables.

- Invest in a sturdy shoulder bag, backpack, or purse with zippers.

- Get locks for your backpack and/or suitcase.

- Keep your backpack and purse on the front side of your body.

- When sitting in a park or restaurant, keep your bag in your sights and/or in your grasp at all times.

- Keep expensive camera equipment, your smartphone, and jewelry hidden when traveling. Only expose valuables when necessary.

- Use credit cards to pay vendors so that any fraudulent transactions may be disputed.

- Travel with as little cash on your person as possible.

- Keep emergency cash in your suitcase should your wallet be stolen.

TAXIS, RIDESHARES, AND PUBLIC TRANSPORTATION

For women travelers, getting around a city can present a number of potential risks. Rideshares and taxis demand that we blindly trust a stranger to drive us to our destination, while women have faced harassment on public transportation around the globe. Thankfully, rideshare apps are rolling out new safety measures and cities are introducing female-only transportation options. Before landing at your destination, research what legitimate taxis look like in that area. For example, New York City's yellow cabs are the only taxis that legally have the right to pick up street-hailing passengers anywhere in the city. Similarly, New York's green cabs are designated by the city to pick up passengers in northern Manhattan and the outer boroughs. When you land in New York, you'll notice unofficial cab companies trying to pick up passengers. These are illegal taxis, not licensed or permitted by the jurisdiction in which they operate. When in doubt about which taxis are legitimate, use apps like Uber or Lyft or contact a car service to order a private pickup. Should you opt for public transportation, be clear on what routes you need to take, ride schedules, and fares.

- When in doubt, take a taxi over public transport, get a private cabin on a train versus a shared cabin, and book a flight that arrives during the day (even if it's more expensive).

- When selecting rideshare programs, be sure to share your location with loved ones so they can track your route.

- If you don't have internet access, make sure your loved ones have a copy of your itinerary and know where you're expected to stay. That way, they can call and check-in.

- Take advantage of airport pickup and drop-offs offered by your hotel.

ANNIKA ZIEHEN

I do take public transport in well-connected cities, but usually only during the day. If there are female-only compartments I will sit there or alternatively seek the company of other women or families. The same goes for longer bus or train rides.

- Only take taxis from taxi stands at the airport and always say you are meeting friends or family, even if you are not.

- When taking public transit alone, it is best to ride during the day.

- If you prefer to see a city on foot, check with other travelers and locals to see what areas are safe and which to avoid.

CAIRO

Both buses and trains can be found in the city catering to women-only passengers. The buses are driven by women.

DELHI

As the number of unaccompanied women traveling to the city increases, women have their own brightly colored train cars and can ride for free.

LONDON

Home to multiple women-only taxi services, the goal is to keep women who travel alone safe, especially at night.

MEXICO CITY

In 2000, trains for women and children were met with a warm reception that spurred the all-female "pink taxi" movement.

RIO DE JANEIRO

Women-only train carriages exist, but the effectiveness is heavily debated due to poor enforcement and victim blaming if a woman is not in the car during rush hours.

TIJUANA

Pink buses equipped with cameras shuttle women, children under twelve, the elderly, and the disabled over a twelve-mile route from the San Ysidro Port of Entry to the eastern end of Tijuana.

TOKYO

Train cars for women and their children are available during rush hours when people are packed closely together and bodily contact is unavoidable.

INTERNATIONAL HOTSPOTS

Thanks to technology, staying connected has never been easier. Regardless of whether you're in a city or exploring a rural village, international hotspots can keep you connected to home and resources. Purchase an international hotspot that you can link to your phone and other Wi-Fi–enabled electronics. Leave your phone on airplane mode with the Wi-Fi on to connect to the hotspot and skip international roaming charges. Many of the hotspots come preloaded with free data, which is perfect for a shorter trip. For longer trips, hotspots offer pay-as-you-go data plans.

"THERE ARE BOTH A WARRIOR AND A CURIOUS CHILD INSIDE OF YOU THAT COME TO THE SURFACE WHEN IMMERSED IN NEW CULTURES. YOU LEARN THINGS ABOUT YOURSELF THAT ONLY THOSE CIRCUMSTANCES COULD HAVE TAUGHT YOU. YOU GIVE PIECES OF YOURSELF TO THE PEOPLE YOU MEET, AND THEY LEAVE PIECES OF THEMSELVES EMBEDDED WITH YOU FOREVER."

EVITA ROBINSON

CREATOR, NOMADNESS TRAVEL
TRIBE AND AUDACITY FEST

ACCOMMODATIONS SAFETY

Before arriving at a new location, research the location as well as your accommodations. You don't need to stay in a fancy hotel to be safe, but it pays to read a few reviews and look out for any safety concerns other women may have raised.

○ Read reviews carefully.

○ Ask friends and family whether they have stayed at a particular hotel before and what their experience was like.

○ Always book a stay in a central location.

○ If booking a hostel, opt for a private room or female-only dorm.

○ Avoid a room on the first floor or garden level.

○ Keep your room number and location private.

○ Keep your window closed and locked overnight.

○ Take advantage of the in-room safe.

○ Lock your suitcases when out of the room.

ANNIKA ZIEHEN

Remember, just because a man reviews a hotel as being safe doesn't mean the same holds true for a woman. Once you arrive, make sure that the lock on your door works, and when sharing a dorm room, always opt for a female-only dorm.

MANAGING ANXIETY
WHILE TRAVELING

Unexpected moments that blur the line between excitement and fear are inevitable when you travel. Whether you're afraid of flying, embarking on your first solo trip, or dealing with an unexpected emergency abroad, anxiety can rear its ugly head at the most inopportune times.

As in all matters of wellness, there isn't a one-size-fits-all solution to fighting anxiety, but once you learn how to access the solid ground inside of you, the whole world opens up. Give the mind a distracting task and it will follow obediently, like a dog that forgets a squirrel in favor of a ball. The following meditative tasks help pull attention away from your anxiety and help bring about a sense of calm. They are exactly what the mind needs in order to pass through a moment of mid-flight turbulence, a wrong turn down an unknown street, or a midnight disturbance deep in the Borneo jungle.

CALMING ANXIETY
ON THE GO

ON-THE-GO MEDITATION
If you're among the third of women who will suffer from an anxiety disorder in her lifetime, you know how patronizing it is when somebody tells you to "just breathe." These simple techniques allow you to regain control and focus on what is in front of you in a more manageable way.

ESME BENJAMIN

Anxiety has always been an undercurrent in my life. Most of the time it doesn't consume too much of my energy, but occasionally the undercurrent becomes a riptide. When that happens, I try to remain buoyant until I'm released, gasping for air and struggling to pull myself back to solid ground. It took me far too many years to learn that the key to squashing anxiety is breathing.

BOX BREATHING

1) Inhale slowly for a count of four.

2) Hold at the top of your breath for the count of four.

3) Exhale slowly for a count of four.

4) Hold at the bottom of your breath for the count of four.

5) Repeat until you feel your stress retreat.

NOTICING

Press your hands together in front of your face or down by your lap. Focus on your hands and feel the temperature of your skin or the pressure of your hands against each other. Internally describe what you notice to keep focused on this one task. For instance, labeling the temperature of your hands as warm, the texture of your skin, and the color of the rings on your fingers will help bring you back to the present moment. This is an easy way to practice noticing. Practice noticing with simple tasks, like brushing your teeth, to help find calm during stressful occurrences throughout the day.

ALTERNATE NOSTRIL BREATHING

1) Raise your right hand to your face and rest the pointer and middle fingers on your forehead.

2) Use your thumb to close the right nostril, inhaling through the left nostril.

3) Release your thumb and close the left nostril with your ring finger.

4) Exhale through the right nostril.

5) Inhale through the right nostril, exhale through the left nostril.

6) Repeat.

COUNTING

Count each inhalation and exhalation until you reach "ten," then start again. If your mind begins to wander and you've unconsciously passed ten, simply come back to "one" without judgment.

5-4-3-2-1 COPING TECHNIQUE

Anxiety can bring feelings of worry, fear, or being overwhelmed. All of these responses are perfectly normal when we travel to new places and experience things outside of our comfort zone. To help you minimize anxiety in a new place, try this coping technique:

- Describe **five** things that you see around you.

- Bring awareness to **four** things you can feel or that are touching you.

- Acknowledge **three** things that you can hear right now.

- Notice **two** smells, either that you like or that you can smell right now.

- Say **one** thing that you like about yourself.

STRIKE A CALMING POSE

After checking into your accommodations, clamber onto the bed, scoot your butt against the headboard, and swing your legs up onto the wall. This drains the lymph fluid and increases circulation, while also giving your hamstrings a nice stretch. Yogis believe it's a calming posture that aids rest, plus it's great for post-flight swollen feet.

"PUT THE FEAR IN YO
LONG ENOUGH TO G
AND GO. ANTICIPAT
AND ANALYSIS PAR
BOTH THE DEATH OF
AND EXPERIENCES
COME TO FRUITION.
YOUR LIFE STORY."

EVITA ROBINSON

CREATOR, NOMADNESS TRAVEL TRIBE
AND AUDACITY FEST

UR BACK POCKET
ET ON THE PLANE
ORY ANXIETY
ALYSIS ARE
SO MANY DREAMS
THAT NEVER
DON'T LET THAT BE

ANTIANXIETY

- Acupressure finger rings, such as the Relax-O-Ring from Saje Natural Wellness

- A lavender oil roll-on when you need calming aromatherapy

- CBD pills or oil for a natural antianxiety option, such as Be Calm from Plant People

- A meditation app, such as Calm or Headspace. Make sure to download the app and preload any meditations ahead of a flight

- A foldable travel yoga mat for practice and relaxing postures on the go

- A journal to practice daily gratitude, practice noticing, and record your thoughts

PACKING LIST

- Your favorite calming teas, such as chamomile or kava

- A weighted eye mask

- If you have the space, a weighted blanket can help with restless sleep

- Calming pillow sprays, such as Sleep Mist by Calm

- Adult coloring book, which can help distract you from your anxiety

- Portable oil diffuser

- Lava rocks are said to offer grounding energy; if you're a believer in energies, a lava rock bracelet could encourage a sense of calm

PRACTICING
SAFE SEX ABROAD

You and your date hit it off? We love to hear it, but it's important to know a country's laws before you take it any further. What starts with PDA and ends with steamy sex can, in some conservative countries, be considered illegal. Read about the country you are visiting beforehand and, as they say, get a room.

SEX AND ACCOMMODATIONS

Prostitution and sex tourism are booming in many countries and laws have been put in place to curb them. These laws don't just apply to male travelers, so make sure to know what is legal and what isn't, especially if you want to "shack up" with a local. In some countries, hotels won't allow unmarried couples, in general, to share a room. In others, you won't be allowed to invite a local back to your bed. If you are legally allowed to share a room, check your hotel's policy on having guests. Usually, you will need to pay the difference from a single to a double room and have your guests check-in with you to avoid any trouble. If you are staying at a hostel dorm, do yourself, and everyone in your room, a favor and get yourself and your date a private room for the night.

SEX AND PROTECTION

In many countries, condoms are readily available at drugstores and pharmacies, but not everywhere. If you are planning on mingling abroad, bring your preferred and trusted brand from home. Whatever your preferred contraception, bring enough of your birth control with you to last through your trip, as you may not be able to find it abroad. In addition, you should speak to your doctor before your trip about any vaccines you might need. Hepatitis B can be prevented with a vaccine, while condoms are a must for protection against Hepatitis C as well as STDs/STIs, including HIV. Many countries offer the morning-after pill over the counter, but you should never assume without checking. The Center for Reproductive Rights gives an overview of global abortion and contraception laws, and is a good source to check when you are already on the road.

VAGINAL HEALTH

Prone to yeast infections? Opt for skirts over pants and bring extra pairs of clean cotton underwear to change frequently. Talk to your gynecologist about antifungal medications like Diflucan, which you can carry with you in case of a yeast or bacterial infection. It's worth bringing a few pH-balanced wipes or a travel-size wash with you too. We love the organic products sold by the female-founded brand Good Clean Love.

IN CASE OF AN EMERGENCY

When traveling to a different country, it pays to spend time getting accustomed to the local laws, rules, and regulations. For example, some conservative countries have special laws when it comes to how women dress, while others have rules about photography. Some laws, like the possession of recreational drugs, can seem like no-brainers, while others, like chewing and spitting out gum in Singapore, are more unknown. To sidestep potential trouble, a mix of preparedness and familiarizing yourself with the local consulate or embassy can prove valuable.

WHAT THE CONSULATE CAN DO

- help you create a plan of action

- contact your family

- provide you with new or replacement passport documents

- provide a birth certificate for your child (if born abroad)

WHAT THE CONSULATE CANNOT DO

- offer legal assistance or service

- investigate a crime

- pay for medical treatment

- issue US police reports

- renew or replace state-issued driver's licenses

IF YOU EXPERIENCE A MEDICAL EMERGENCY ON YOUR TRIP

- Scout out medical provider and pharmacy locations.

- Call your current insurance provider and ask about coverage in your destination.

- Purchase travel insurance (see page 122) and consider evacuation insurance.

- Know the symbol of pharmacies in your destination country. A green plus sign in France indicates where to get medication, whereas the same symbol in the United States directs you to a marijuana dispensary.

- Keep a list of your allergies and medications handy at all times.

- Call your insurer as soon as possible to avoid paying out of pocket.

IF YOU EXPERIENCE SEXUAL ABUSE OR HARASSMENT WHILE TRAVELING

- Remember that whatever happened was not your fault.

- Prioritize your health and seek medical attention if necessary.

- Contact your embassy or consulate. They will be able to help you navigate the situation from a legal and logistical standpoint.

- Seek guidance from other female travelers or local women. Many female travel groups (see resources) help women navigate difficult situations and can point you in the right direction.

- Legal and medical care vary country-by-country; be aware that filing a police report might not be your safest option. This is another reason to seek guidance from a consulate and other women.

- You may need to process what has happened from an emotional standpoint. Turn to online therapy apps, such as Talkspace or BetterHelp, to speak with licensed counselors.

IF YOU ARE ROBBED

- File a police report, which is necessary for your travel insurance.

- Reach out to family who can wire money via PayPal, Venmo, Western Union, or Xoom.

- If your passport is lost or stolen, immediately call the National Passport Center to register it as lost, then go to the nearest consulate or embassy.

TRAVEL SAFE

○ Pack a personalized first aid kit, including any essential medication.

○ Bring pH-balanced wipes to maintain optimal vaginal health on the go.

○ Download the official US State Department Smart Traveler app, which shares frequently updated travel advisories, alerts, and country-specific warnings.

○ Write down the contact information for the local embassy, police, and tourist police.

○ Lock up any valuables in a safety deposit box.

○ Purchase locks for your luggage.

TY CHECKLIST

○ Download the BSafe app, which allows you to share your location with a network of friends, family, and coworkers. Unlike other location-sharing services, BSafe offers additional tools like live streaming, voice activation, an SOS button, and more.

○ Have your accommodation address written down in the local language.

○ If heading out, always make sure you know the best way to get back to your accommodations.

○ Jot down key phrases you'll need to help you communicate any allergies or medical conditions.

○ Print and email yourself a copy of your passport in case it is stolen.

TRAVELING AS A MODERN WOMAN

The experience of traveling doesn't just differ between men and women, it also varies for people of color and LGBTQIA+ travelers. Women of color often face discrimination beyond their gender as well as experience outright racism both stateside and internationally, while LGBTQIA+ travelers can be confronted with violence for simply showing affection in public. While these unfair discriminations can create extra obstacles to sidestep, these expert tips will help ensure every person can make the most of their travels.

TRAVELERS OF COLOR

KNOW BEFORE YOU GO

"Forewarned is forearmed." Being aware of what you may experience as a traveler of color will prepare you for potential experiences on your trip. How are people of color (POC) perceived in Russia, for instance? How may the current political situation in, say, Switzerland potentially affect POC? Lean on social media for up-to-date reports, testimonies, and accounts from other travelers. Ahead of your trip, look to connect with other POC communities (see resources), such as NOMADNESS Travel Tribe and Latinas Who Travel. The more knowledge you have of a destination and what to expect, the better you can prepare.

BE PREPARED FOR NEGATIVE ATTENTION, BUT DON'T EXPECT IT

Your research has led you to discover that people of color have experienced racial discrimination while in Australia; what now? Just because it happened to others does not necessarily mean it will be your own experience. Don't allow what you read or hear to taint your perception of a destination without actually meeting the people or experiencing the culture for yourself. While it's important to arm yourself with knowledge ahead of a trip, don't let it dictate your experience. Go in with an open heart and a positive mindset.

YOU DON'T HAVE TO BE AN AMBASSADOR FOR ALL TRAVELERS OF COLOR

Don't feel as though you have to answer questions about your skin color, religious affiliation, political leanings, or anything else. You are under no obligation to satisfy other people's curiosity surrounding race. While educating the masses is great, it should not come at the detriment of your personal safety, mental well-being, emotional health, or having a good time.

ONEIKA RAYMOND

I've had my skin and hair touched without permission in South Korea, been asked for my autograph in Poland, and caused a fender bender in Mexico because the driver was too busy staring at me instead of keeping an eye on the road. I've been called Michelle Obama in the Philippines, had my picture taken without consent in Uzbekistan, and been racially profiled in Ecuador. Depending on where you are in the world, it's been my experience that being a traveler with black or brown skin gets you noticed.

CONNECT WITH LIKE-MINDED TRAVELERS OF COLOR

Whether it's for information, advice, or simply to swap stories, sometimes connecting with those who share a common ethnicity or culture can help you better enjoy yourself on the road. You can connect with other travelers of color in various countries and cities by simply approaching them and initiating a conversation. Another way is to search for travel groups catering to POC or to connect with other travelers of color in your destination via social media. As wonderful as it is to travel to foreign lands, seeing a familiar face can be integral to your enjoyment and exploration of a new country or city.

DESTINATIONS FOR TRAVELERS OF COLOR

JAPAN

There are so many reasons to love Japan: The country boasts stunning scenery, amazing food, interesting history, and mind-blowing fashion. The country's deep appreciation for African American and Afro-Caribbean culture is particularly intriguing. Here, you'll find nightclubs spinning the latest hip-hop and dancehall reggae music all over Tokyo, as well as Japanese B-boys and dancehall queens.

SOUTH AFRICA

South Africa's history of apartheid is a tragic one, but the cultural renaissance taking place in cities like Johannesburg make it a must-visit for travelers of color. Johannesburg's Maboneng district is one of the hippest in the city and is bursting with creatives making waves in the art and cultural scene. Even if you're not into the arts, the low cost of living, combined with the abundance of beaches and wildlife, make this country an attractive vacation spot for tourists who are keen on adventure.

BRAZIL

Going to Brazil can feel a bit like going home for the traveler of color. Its largely multiracial population means that you're more likely to blend in with the locals, avoiding the stares and harassment that can occur when traveling to nations where there's a dearth of diversity. Beyond enjoying the gorgeous sights and wonderful music, you can explore the large and vibrant Afro-Brazilian communities in Salvador de Bahia and the Japanese-Brazilian communities in São Paulo.

JAMAICA

This gorgeous Caribbean island is known for its rich history, reggae music, and cuisine. Considered one of the more laid-back and popular islands in the Caribbean, Jamaica has just about something for everyone. From rest and relaxation at one of the many beachfront resorts to floating down the Martha Brae River on a bamboo raft, this island satisfies most traveler's needs. For travelers of color, Jamaica is especially welcoming and hospitable.

"I'M BLACK, I'VE ALWAYS BEEN BLACK, I'LL ALWAYS BE BLACK. I CAN ONLY MOVE THROUGH THE WORLD AS A BLACK PERSON, AND I HAVE TRAVELED TO EVERY COUNTRY IN THE WORLD. JUST BECAUSE YOU HEAR ONE OR TWO NEGATIVE STORIES FROM SOMEONE DOES NOT MEAN YOU SHOULD WRITE A COUNTRY OFF YOUR BUCKET LIST."

JESSICA NABONGO

TRAVEL WRITER
AND TRAVEL EXPERT

LGBTQIA+ TRAVELERS

For travelers who identify as LGBTQIA+, traveling can present its own set of challenges. From booking hotel rooms for you and your partner, to navigating laws around public displays of affection, there are many things to consider.

FAMILIARIZE YOURSELF WITH LOCAL LGBTQIA+ LAWS

There are a lot of countries where same-sex relationships between men are punished, while same-sex relationships between women are not. There are countries where any same-sex acts are considered illegal and can result in dire consequences. For example, Antigua considers same-sex acts illegal with up to fifteen years prison time as punishment. It is important to do your homework before your trip. Find out how LGBTQIA+ people are treated in the destination you're traveling to and how other travelers have experienced traveling in that particular country.

KNOW WHAT COUNTRIES TO AVOID AS AN LGBTQIA+ TRAVELER

While you are free to travel around the globe, it's important to know which countries are considered the most dangerous for LGBTQIA+-identifying travelers. Countries like Qatar and Saudi Arabia are very conservative and operate under Sharia Law. Homosexuality is punished in Qatar by flogging, prison time, and even the death penalty. In other countries like Tanzania or Nigeria, same-sex acts (particularly between men) can result in prison time. If you are keen on traveling to these more conservative nations, it is advised to be discreet. Or consider traveling instead to one of the twenty-eight countries that support same-sex marriage.

THE REALITIES OF CHECKING INTO A HOTEL WITH YOUR PARTNER

After a long day of traveling, retiring to your hotel room is a welcome respite. However, checking in can be uncomfortable when you asked for one bed to share with your partner and were instead given two. Depending on the laws of where you are visiting, this miscommunication can be easily resolved with a frank conversation. We recommend booking a stay at LGBTQIA+-friendly or -owned hotels (see resources), where same-sex couples are both welcomed and celebrated.

DESTINATIONS FOR LGBTQIA+ TRAVELERS

VIENNA

Located in Austria, this beautiful European city is known as the music capital of the world. It is here that some of the most influential composers—including Mozart, Salieri, Schubert, Haydn, and Vivaldi—got their start. Come to Vienna for its architecture and cuisine (especially the world-famous chocolate cake: Sachertorte). For same-sex couples, Vienna is particularly welcoming. For lesbian travelers, head to the Frauencafé, a woman-founded café that has been operating since the 1970s, or for a night out, check out PiNKED, a night club that hosts women-only clubbing sessions.

DANI HEINRICH

The words "I'm gay" are still hard to say. As a femme lesbian, when I travel I am often met with the dreaded question: "Do you have a boyfriend?" And I have to come out all over again. Coming out is stressful each and every time, because I never know what the reaction to it will be. Will it get awkward? Will someone make a homophobic comment? Will there be an uncomfortable silence? In my experience, even if everyone generally reacts well, traveling as a lesbian can come with challenges.

COSTA RICA

Costa Rica was the first Central American country to legalize same-sex marriage, making it one of the more progressive countries you can visit in this part of the world. From its pristine beaches to its rainforests, Costa Rica is known for its biodiversity and wealth of wildlife. Adventure travelers and nature lovers can't go wrong with traveling to this rugged country with coastlines on the Caribbean and the Pacific Ocean. For same-sex couples, check out Manuel Antonio National Park, which is home to gay beaches and LGBTQIA+-friendly resorts and hotels.

PROVINCETOWN, MASSACHUSETTS

Provincetown is an iconic LGBTQIA+ vacation spot. For lesbian travelers, there are about ten female-centric events held throughout the year, making this open-minded community an attractive option for queer women. Provincetown has more lesbian-owned businesses per capita than any other place in the United States, the highest concentration of same-sex households in the country, and many LGBTQIA+-owned B&Bs and inns. The daily tea dance at the Boatslip—an expansive deck that overlooks Provincetown's West End Harbor—is something every LGBTQIA+ traveler has to experience at least once.

NEW ZEALAND

This island country in the southwestern Pacific Ocean has long been considered a top LGBTQIA+-friendly destination. New Zealand was the first in the region to enact same-sex marriage and is consistently rated one of the more inclusive countries to visit. Because of its visible and open LGBTQIA+ scene, cities like Auckland are extremely welcoming to same-sex couples. There you'll find a slew of bars, festivals, venues, and events catering to the LGBTQIA+ community, including an annual Pride Week held each February. Beyond Auckland, New Zealand boasts stunning scenery and endless outdoor adventure activities.

"THE LGBTQIA+ COMMUNITY IS NOT A MONOLITHIC GROUP—WE'RE MADE OF SEPARATE AND SOMETIMES OVERLAPPING COMMUNITIES WITH DISTINCT CULTURES AND HISTORIES."

MEG TEN EYCK
CEO, EVERYQUEER

PUERTO RICO

If you don't want to travel too far from the United States, this tropical destination doesn't even require a passport. Because of its status as a United States commonwealth country, the legal rights of LGBTQIA+ citizens has had a great influence on Puerto Rico, which is now the queer-friendliest of all Caribbean nations. Both San Juan and Ponce have several LGBTQIA+ friendly bars and nightclubs. While there aren't any dedicated lesbian bars per se, the go-to place is El Cojo, a bar in the Hato Rey district. Of course, Puerto Rico's gay bars welcome women.

A quick ferry ride will bring you to the island of Vieques, which is famous for Mosquito Bay—one of the most bioluminescent bays in the world. Don't expect any LGBTQIA+ nightlife, but you will find serene beaches, unspoiled nature, and wild horses roaming freely. If you're looking for a relaxing hideaway or a lesbian-friendly wedding spot on the island, the W Retreat & Spa in Vieques offers same-sex ceremonies.

NEW YORK CITY

It should come as no surprise that NYC is a prime destination for LGBTQIA+ travelers. It is here, in this iconic city, that the Stonewall riots kicked off the gay liberation movement in 1969. NYC is known for being a veritable melting pot of cultures, ethnicities, sexual orientation, ideologies, beliefs, and styles. For LGBTQIA+ travelers, you'll find some real gems from LGBTQIA+-owned bars and shops to popular spots like Big Gay Ice Cream, Cult Party, and Babeland.

PREGNANT AND MOMMY TRAVELERS

Be it a fear of glowering stares over your crying baby or the worries around traveling in your third trimester, too often moms and moms-to-be are deterred from traveling. As a new mom, it can seem like your options for travel are limited, but that is far from true. Modern mommies are taking "babymoons" and raising their children to be international jetsetters before the age of ten! Whether you're six months pregnant or a mom to a six-month-old, travel is a luxury you can still enjoy as long as you're prepared.

DECIDING WHEN TO TRAVEL WHILE PREGNANT

It is widely believed that traveling in the second trimester of pregnancy is safest. If you plan to travel in your third trimester, first check with your ob-gyn to ensure it is safe to do so. Next, check with the airlines or cruises you may be taking as some will refuse service to a woman in her third trimester of pregnancy. As a rule of thumb, you should aim to complete your travels before your thirty-sixth week of pregnancy.

NIKKI VARGAS

I'll never forget solo traveling in Uruguay in my early twenties. I was sitting on a Colonia-bound ferry when I spotted a couple traveling with their baby. Up until that point, I had assumed family travel to be something limited to Disney World vacations and kid-friendly resorts. Yet here was a pair of backpacking parents with a newborn in tow! It just goes to show you, there is no one way to travel as a mom or mom-to-be.

PICKING A PREGNANCY-SAFE DESTINATION

If you are pregnant it is best to avoid humid climates and steer clear of areas known to carry the Zika virus or yellow fever. Similarly, if you are far along in your pregnancy it is wise to avoid remote locations should you require medical attention. Some destinations require vaccinations for measles, mumps, and rubella. Because these viruses contain live cultures, always check with your doctor beforve getting any travel vaccinations. When choosing your accommodations, always opt for a location that is conveniently located near eateries and attractions, so as to cut down the amount of time you're on your feet.

TRAVELING WHILE PREGNANT

Avoid heavy bags and always opt for a roller bag. When flying, aim for an aisle seat so you can stretch your legs often and have access to the bathroom with little effort. If you did not book an aisle seat in advance, talk with the gate agent prior to boarding as they often accommodate pregnant passengers. For long cruises, there is typically a medical team on board for any unforeseen emergencies. Double-check that is in fact the case prior to booking your cruise, lest you're caught at sea without a doctor. Throughout your travels, no matter your mode of transportation, remember to stretch often, wear loose clothing, drink lots of fluids, and wear compression socks to help avoid deep vein thrombosis (DVT), a blood clot in the veins.

PREPARING FOR LABOR

While it is not recommended to travel toward the end of your third trimester, if you do so, it is crucial to know the phone number and locations of the closest hospitals. Make sure that your health or travel insurance covers pregnancy and labor abroad, as this can incur exorbitant costs. If you are traveling abroad, keep the number of the nearest embassy or consulate available so that you can obtain a passport for your newborn.

GETTING THROUGH AIRPORT SECURITY

The best advice for getting through airport security while pregnant or with small kids is to give yourself plenty of time. If you are pregnant and concerned about walking through the screening technology, the TSA recommends requesting a pat-down instead. For moms with small kids, snacks make every flight more enjoyable. Knowing the rules around food will make security a breeze. Pack food in easy-to-access places as some security checkpoints will ask that they be removed and scanned just as toiletries would. For infants and toddlers, you can bring more than 3.4 ounces of formula, breast milk, and juice through security. Be sure to take out these liquids so that you are not pulled out of line for additional screening. These liquids get scanned separately and may be subject to additional screening.

FLYING WITH A NEWBORN

If traveling with an infant, pick a seat at the front of the cabin and ask for one of the in-flight bassinets offered to passengers on long-haul flights. If flying on a shorter flight, always choose an aisle seat for easy bathroom access and extra room. While most airlines allow infants to travel for free on their mother's lap, some airlines do charge additional fees. Check with your airline ahead of time.

WHAT YOU NEED TO KNOW ABOUT TRAVELING WITH STROLLERS

For moms with small children, you can bring your stroller through security. Ideally, your stroller should be able to fold up and fit through the scanning machine, otherwise it will need to be inspected separately by a TSA agent. Most airlines are stroller-friendly and do not count them as standard baggage. On some airlines, such as Delta, you can gate-check larger strollers for free before boarding, while smaller strollers can be brought into the cabin.

WHAT TO PACK IN YOUR CARRY-ON BAG

As tempting as it may be to pack a lifetime supply of diapers and formula, resist the urge. Pack only what is absolutely necessary in your carry-on to help lighten your load. If traveling with toddlers, having a small "bag of tricks" is crucial to keeping the kiddos entertained during long layovers and flights. This "bag of tricks" can have anything from coloring books to small toys to stickers— just make sure it doesn't take up too much space or weight in your carry-on.

BREASTFEEDING WHILE TRAVELING

If you are uncomfortable breastfeeding in public, many domestic and Canadian airports now offer breastfeeding pods thanks to the women-owned company Mamava. Download the Mamava app, which points you in the direction of thousands of breastfeeding pods and lactation spaces. If you're unable to breastfeed ahead of your flight, you can breastfeed onboard. US legislation protects the rights of mothers to breastfeed, and breastfeeding in public places in the United Kingdom is protected under the 2010 Equality Act. Although breastfeeding practices differ slightly by airline, the rights of mothers to breastfeed are largely recognized. If you prefer not to breastfeed on board, most airplanes have allowances for breast milk, formula, and baby food, which they will warm up for you.

GETTING A CRIB AT YOUR HOTEL

Whether you are staying at a hotel or Airbnb-like accommodations, request a crib (if available) ahead of time to ensure you can put the little one down for a nap upon arrival. You can also invest in purchasing a collapsible travel crib, such as the highly recommended Nuna SENA Aire Travel Crib.

"THE BABY FOOD, THE PACK AND PLAY, THE DIAPERS. IT'S EASY TO FORGET THAT EVERY COUNTRY HAS ITS OWN SOLUTIONS FOR THOSE THINGS. WHAT A NEAT WAY TO DISCOVER A LITTLE BIT MORE ABOUT THE WORLD BY EXPERIENCING THE LIFESTYLES OF OTHER PARENTS."

BETH SANTOS
FOUNDER AND CEO,
WANDERFUL

PREGNANCY PACKING LIST

- Carry-on bag with wheels
- Lumbar pillow
- Neck pillow
- Reflux medications
- Healthy, high-protein snack like nuts
- Compression socks
- Comfortable slip-on shoes
- Flowy maxi skirts
- Stretchy leggings

- Bump band
- Panty liners
- Extra water
- Anti-nausea wristbands
- Anti-nausea medications
- A doctor's note, which some airlines will ask for if you're further along in your pregnancy
- Prenatal vitamins
- Pregnancy-safe sunscreen

TRAVELING
DURING YOUR PERIOD

The first step to handling your period abroad is knowing what to pack. While pads can be found just about anywhere in the world, tampons may be harder to come by. If traveling abroad during your period, the products below are essential.

PACK A MENSTRUAL CUP

Travelers who menstruate swear by menstrual cups, which collect your period for up to twelve hours and offer a more environmentally friendly option than traditional pads or tampons. While in a private bathroom, simply dump the cup and rinse it out before reusing. If you are on the go, use toilet paper to wipe the cup down and wet naps for your hands before leaving the stall.

AVOID LEAKS WITH PERIOD-PROOF UNDERWEAR

Leak-proof period underwear, such as those sold by Thinx, takes away the stress of traveling during your period. Both cute and functional, these panties can hold up to five tampons' worth of liquid. Make sure you will have access to running water to rinse them out at the end of the day.

SKIPPING A PERIOD WITH BIRTH CONTROL

Many female travelers use birth control to manipulate or skip their periods while traveling in remote places such as the Sahara Desert. Some brands of birth control even reduce the number of periods you have a year. If you are thinking of using your birth control to alter your menstruation cycle or skip a period, be sure to first consult your gynecologist.

TRAVELING
WITH MENOPAUSE

From hot flashes to insomnia, traveling with menopause presents its own set of challenges for women of a certain age. Don't let fears of suffering hot flashes on the plane and managing mood swings abroad deter you from a well-deserved vacation.

KEEP YOUR COOL WHILE TRAVELING

Because hot flashes can strike at any moment, selecting a destination that is not at the zenith of heat during your trip will make for a more pleasurable experience. If you do choose a warm destination, make sure your hotel has a pool, is close to the beach, or has a shower in your room for a quick cool-down. Whether you're on a transatlantic flight or an overnight train, hot flashes can strike at inopportune times. Wear a loose cotton shirt and always travel with a handheld fan and/or face mist to help you cool down on the go.

AVOID YOUR TRIGGERS

Perhaps your hot flashes come after a spicy meal. Maybe you get hit with a hot flash during the midday heat. Take note of what triggers hot flashes in your home life and try to avoid those triggers while on the road.

MAKE SURE YOU HAVE AIR ONBOARD

As soon as you board the plane, make sure your seat's ventilation fan is working. Having that fan is crucial for cooling down during any midair hot flashes you might experience. If your seat's fan is not working, speak to a flight attendant about switching seats.

GET MOVING WITH SOME EXERCISE

Exercise is known to help menopause symptoms, so take thirty minutes and hit your hotel gym or go for a jog. While working up a sweat to prevent hot flashes might seem counterproductive, studies do show that women who are active tend to have fewer hot flashes.

BRING PERSONAL LUBRICANT

For women going through menopause, vaginal dryness can be a painful symptom. Female-owned company Good Clean Love offers pH-balanced personal lubricants for vaginal dryness.

GET A GOOD NIGHT'S SLEEP

Sometimes insomnia and menopause unfortunately go hand in hand. Help yourself get rest by packing a sleep mask, lavender spray for your pillow, and melatonin.

"TRAVELING AS A WOMAN HAS AWAKENED A SENSE OF CONFIDENCE IN WHAT I CAN DO AND WHO I CAN BECOME."

STEPHANIE FLOR

FOUNDER,
AROUND THE WORLD BEAUTY

GOING
SOLO

WHAT TO EXPECT
WHEN
SOLO TRAVELING

When it comes to solo traveling, the idea of exploring a country alone can sometimes prove daunting. But once you pop open that proverbial can of worms, you will be introduced to a style of travel that is all about self-discovery and self-care. Spending weeks on end by yourself is a really quick way to get to know yourself. Time alone forces you to rethink everything and challenge how you see the world. You will relish breaking the boundaries you have set for yourself, make huge steps in personal growth, and walk away with new perspectives that can only be gained from learning to love yourself. Whether it's your first time solo traveling or your twentieth, venturing into the world alone comes with a few common themes.

BROOKE SAWARD

As much as I love sharing my adventures with people close to me, solo travel is still my favorite way to see the world. I think the freedom of solo travel is what draws me in: The ability to spend hours on end admiring modern art or to sleep in past noon if my body needs it. There's nothing quite like the freedom of exploring a new city on your own and catering to your own interests.

YOU WILL REDISCOVER YOUR LIKES AND DISLIKES

As a solo traveler you'll learn the inherent pleasure of building your day around what you *want* to do instead of what you *have* to do. You'll quickly discover what excites you and what doesn't—be it exploring art galleries, going on a hike, or indulging in wine tastings.

IT'S OKAY IF YOU DON'T LIKE SOLO TRAVELING

There are so many factors that will determine how you experience your own journey: the destination you choose, what is happening in your life at the moment, how much contact you have with friends and family back home, and how willing you are to immerse yourself in the present. You don't have to love solo travel, but it's worth trying at least once in your life to challenge yourself, to learn, and to grow.

EXPERT TIPS
FOR SOLO FEMALE TRAVELERS

CHOOSE A DESTINATION THAT WORKS FOR YOU

Where you decide to travel will dictate the type of trip you have, so it is important to be honest with yourself in deciding what you are traveling for (take the quiz on pages 12–13). Traveling after a breakup? You might want to avoid couple-centric locations like the Maldives, Fiji, and Paris. In need of a break from the chaos of work? You might consider a trip to the mountains to reconnect with nature and disconnect with your email. Looking forward to meeting other travelers? Head to Europe.

NIKKI VARGAS

Landing in Buenos Aires by myself, I felt as if I wanted to crawl into my skin and hide. The realization that I was alone in an entire country was humbling, to say the least. Not a single person in Argentina knew who I was or cared about my well-being; I was the only one who could and would hold my hand, lift my spirits, and comfort my fears. In a nutshell, I learned a lot about empowerment and self-sufficiency on my first-ever solo trip.

"ACT LIKE A LOCAL AND EXUDE CONFIDENCE. IT'S A NEW DESTINATION, SO IT'S TOTALLY NATURAL TO FEEL JITTERY AND LOST AT TIMES. BUT IF YOU WANT TO DETER UNWANTED ATTENTION, I'VE LEARNED THAT IT ALWAYS HELPS TO SEEM INVULNERABLE."

AILEEN ADALID

TRAVEL WRITER,
IAMAILEEN.COM

BROOKE SAWARD

I hate to be a cliché, but if I knew then what I know now, I'd have gotten where I am quicker, easier, and with more money in my pockets. But it was through all of those mistakes—the times I was conned by cab-drivers or forgot my passport on a train—that I learned everything can be figured out.

BOOK ACCOMMODATIONS IN ADVANCE

As exciting as it may sound to land in Bali and simply "wing it," after a long flight you'll be grateful to know you have a guaranteed place to rest your head at night. Regardless of your travel style, it is a good idea to always book at least the first night of accommodations before you arrive in a new city. If you are traveling solo for the first time, we would go so far as to recommend booking all of your accommodations ahead of time so you have the comfort of knowing where you'll be staying every step of the way.

SHARE YOUR ITINERARY WITH FRIENDS AND FAMILY

Leave a copy of your itinerary with your loved ones back home; that way if no one hears from you for a while, they can try to make contact another way—trust us, it will make everyone feel better. By the same token, it is always a good idea to let these same people know if you are planning to go offline or off the grid for a while, so you don't cause alarm.

WAKE UP EARLY

If you are visiting a city that has a lot of attractions to tick off your list, make use of your early starts by getting in line at monuments at least fifteen minutes before opening time. That way you will find yourself first in the door and can enjoy the quiet solitude of these magical moments.

BUY TRAVELER'S INSURANCE

Travel insurance is an easy way to alleviate some pre-trip stress because you know you'll be covered. Travel insurance typically falls into two categories: medical and trip cancellation. First check with your current health insurance company to see if they cover injuries or medical evacuations abroad. Otherwise, you can purchase medical travel insurance to cover you for the duration of your travels. Trip cancellation coverage can help recoup costs associated with lost baggage, missed or canceled flights, et cetera. When considering travel insurance, be sure to compare all the plans available as prices and inclusions can vary based on the country you're visiting.

BROOKE SAWARD

My favorite time of day to explore a city is at first light. Aside from the natural beauty of starting each day early, it is also the best time to avoid large crowds. Even during high season, I have enjoyed Paris all to myself before my fellow travelers are even awake.

KELLY LEWIS

There are a million things that solo traveling has taught me, but above all else, it's that people are inherently good and that we are all interconnected. You can find yourself in some pretty unexpected situations while you travel, but in the end, surviving those situations gives you a feeling of accomplishment that allows you to make peace with yourself and the less glamorous parts of your life.

TRAVEL ALONE BUT NOT LONELY

Traveling solo is a great way to meet people and engage with interesting strangers. But let's say you fancy yourself more of an introvert than an extrovert. If the idea of approaching a stranger at a café feels overwhelming, then make some connections before you arrive. Ask friends and family if they have any contacts in the city you are traveling to who would be interested in showing you around. You can also lean on women-only online groups (see resources) that connect female travelers.

CHALLENGE YOURSELF WITH DAILY GOALS

If you are finding solo travel isolating, a great way to distract yourself—and allow yourself to get into the groove of solo travel—is to give yourself daily challenges. This can be anything from challenging yourself to strike up a conversation with a stranger, ordering dinner entirely in French, or finally visiting that neighborhood that's been on your list of places to see. This is a great way to task yourself with different focuses and really immerse yourself in your surroundings.

LEARN A NEW SKILL

Another way to make the most of where you are is to learn a new skill specific to that location. If you're visiting Paris, you can opt for a pastry-making class; if you're traveling through Guatemala, you can visit one of the female artisan co-ops to learn the art of Mayan weaving. Learning a skill helps connect you to a country in a unique way.

ALLOW YOURSELF TO WANDER

Allow yourself to discover a new coffee shop that hasn't hit the hipster lists yet or to find a small bookstore you can get lost in for hours. Getting lost is all part of the journey to finding yourself.

"AS WOMEN, WE ARE CONSTANTLY BEING JUDGED. WE ARE TOLD HOW TO LOOK, HOW TO ACT, WHAT TO FEEL, WHAT TO STAND FOR. SOLO TRAVELING STRIPS THAT AWAY AND ALLOWS US TO GET DOWN TO OUR INNERMOST TRUTHS. WE BECOME STRONGER WOMEN."

VALERIE JOY WILSON

TRAVEL EXPERT, FOUNDER OF
TRUSTED TRAVEL GIRL

BROOKE SAWARD

I was twenty years old when I first traveled solo. I was young and desperate for adventure. My life up to that point had been quite sheltered and limited to the environment I grew up in, so I was enticed by the unknown. As much as it is a state of being, solo travel has become my preferred style. It has molded me into the woman I am today.

DESTINATIONS FOR SOLO FEMALE TRAVELERS

JAPAN

From the women-only rooms available in many hostels to the women-only cars offered in some trains during peak hours, Japan is one of the safest countries you can visit. Here you'll find women-only buses, capsule hotels with gender-specific floors, and a bullet train that will whisk you away to cities like Tokyo and Kyoto. Most written signs are in both Japanese and English, so don't be deterred by the language. Japan is both easy to navigate and affordable for solo travelers. Visit in April for cherry blossom season.

THE NETHERLANDS

When you think of the Netherlands, you most likely think of Amsterdam, but there is so much to see beyond the capital city. Being a small country geographically, the Netherlands is easy to get around by train, safe for solo travelers, and, best of all, it is bursting with colors, culture, and Dutch cuisine.

NEW ZEALAND

If you are looking for a solo destination that packs in a little more adventure, look no further than New Zealand. This island nation has quickly made its way to the top of many travelers' lists given its epic landscapes, ample offerings for day hikers, and road-tripping appeal. Start your journey in Queenstown, where you'll meet other backpackers and solo travelers. From there, you can join adventure tours, choose between staying at campsites or lodgings, or rent a car to venture out on your own. If the idea of traveling around New Zealand alone gives you pause, there are plenty of women-only activities, day trips, and group tours offered through Women's Adventure NZ.

ANNIKA ZIEHEN

Some people have a list of solo travel destinations, but personally I don't buy into the concept. Rather than following a strict schedule of places to visit, I think with any trip you need to follow your heart and do what excites you. The beauty of a solo trip is that you don't need to take anyone into consideration but yourself. There is no need to compromise—enjoy that freedom.

ONEIKA RAYMOND

When I look back at all the amazing things I've had the chance to see and do in my life, I'm filled with an immense sense of gratitude. I've visited nearly 120 countries—6 of which I have lived and worked in—and have seen world wonders spanning from the Great Wall of China to the verdant peaks of Machu Picchu. I've made lifelong friends in Mexico, had life-changing experiences in South Africa, and even met the love of my life while traveling.

IRELAND

Ireland is a great destination for solo travelers. For starters, English is widely spoken there, making this country easy to navigate. Ireland is also easy to get to with an international airport serving Dublin and relatively short flights from the United States' and Canada's east coasts. The other big draw for solo travelers is the friendliness and hospitality of the Irish. Grab a seat at a local pub, order a pint, and in no time you'll find yourself making new friends from all ages and walks of life.

ICELAND

Known as the land of fire and ice, Iceland is one of the world's most sought-after destinations. For solo female travelers, Iceland is considered the safest country for women to travel, thanks to a low crime rate, solid infrastructure, and strong sense of hospitality. Because of its many natural wonders—from hot springs to geysers to lava fields—Iceland's Golden Circle has become a hot spot for travelers looking to explore the country's beauty in a matter of days. For solo travelers, choose between renting a car when you arrive at Keflavík airport or joining one of the many day trips that depart from Reykjavík to the Golden Circle. Plan on staying at least five days there to explore both Reykjavík and the nearby natural attractions.

HOW TO MAKE
POSITIVE
ABROAD

A IMPACT

LET'S TALK ABOUT
SUSTAINABLE TRAVEL

Sustainable travel aims to solve the question of how a destination can support tourism without damaging its natural or cultural environment in the long run. While tourism can help revitalize a local economy and bring jobs to a community, it can also negatively impact a country in many ways, including damaging the landscape, increasing pollution, and straining local resources.

The old adage of "take only memories, leave only footprints" is perhaps the best way to describe the aim of sustainable travel and how the onus falls on each individual traveler to respect the destination they are visiting. Being a responsible traveler encompasses everything from sustainability on the road to practicing respect for other cultures to how we connect with wildlife.

ELISE FITZSIMMONS

I have found that committing to a few sustainable practices when I travel, like carrying a water bottle with a UV light, makes traveling sustainably easier to achieve. See if you can change one little thing on every trip you take. Swapping your tampons for a menstrual cup, packing your own metal straw, and bringing a foldable tote for daily purchases all cut down on single-use items.

TIPS ON SUSTAINABLE TRAVEL

CUT CARBON EMISSIONS BY REDUCING AIR TRAVEL

Cruise ships and planes are the biggest polluters when it comes to traveling. Air travel has become cheaper over the years and many new airlines have popped up offering lower airfares. With this development, more people can afford to travel by plane, much to the detriment of the environment. If you consider yourself a responsible traveler, consider your impact on the environment when you fly. At a minimum, you should offset your carbon footprint for each flight. These days, many airlines offer carbon emission offset programs that allow travelers to pay an extra fee when booking to plant a tree.

Because flying is often unavoidable in order to travel, it is important to reduce the number of flights you take and make sure you make the most of each flight. That means taking longer trips and traveling more slowly when you can. Keep in mind that you pay the same for a flight whether you stay a week or a month, so make the most of it.

CONSIDER TRAIN OR BUS TRAVEL

For distances where you don't have to cross an ocean, there are buses and trains. Train travel is fun, especially in many South and Southeast Asian destinations and across Europe. Many countries are connected with a reliable transit network, so it is not only easy but cheaper to forgo a plane.

ELISE FITZSIMMONS

Traveling by train is, by far, my favorite way to travel—it gives me the chance to collect my thoughts, plan, and admire the countryside. The Zephyr across western America, the Trans-Siberian through Mongolia and China, and the TGV across France all have their own unique charms and amenities, while offering a rotating cast of cabinmates. The rules of engagement are different for each train and each culture. For example, "train friends" in Russia are strangers who share a cabin, confide deeply personal intimacies, and are bonded for the duration of the ride, only to never see each other again.

BEING A RESPONSIBLE
TRAVELER

PACK MINDFULLY

There are several ways to minimize your environmental impact while traveling, and they are not too different from what you might already be practicing at home. Choose reusable products such as solid shampoos that can be stored in tin containers. We tend to use a lot more plastic bottles when we travel than at home, and many countries don't have proper recycling facilities. Avoid adding to the mountain of trash by using a water bottle that can filter tap or natural water from a stream or lake. It removes harmful bacteria and is a cost-effective way to get drinking water without having to keep spending money on bottled water.

SUPPORT LOCAL BUSINESSES

One of the best ways to practice responsible travel is to be conscious about how you are spending your money. Putting your dollars toward locally owned businesses and eco-conscious hotels can help support the economy. If shopping for food, look to purchase produce grown in the region from places such as farmers' markets. If shopping for souvenirs, opt to buy goods from local artisans instead of mass-produced items in novelty shops.

BEING MINDFUL OF OTHER CULTURES

When you travel, you're visiting someone else's home and have to adjust to their rules. What does it mean to be mindful of other people and their cultures? It varies by country and usually a travel guidebook will give you a good indication of the dos and don'ts of a specific destination. While a country's laws and regulations don't have to make sense to you, remember that you are a guest and need to follow them. Rules can include anything from dress codes to tipping culture to how to speak on a country's politics or current affairs. In Thailand, for example, it is unacceptable to speak ill of the king.

Especially when visiting religious sites, you will need to adhere to a certain dress code, and in some countries, you have to take your shoes off when entering someone's home or business. While in countries like Morocco you don't need to cover up by law, dressing more conservatively is much appreciated by the locals.

BE A COURTEOUS PHOTOGRAPHER

For many travelers, sweeping landscapes, ancient buildings, and the faces of the locals are a photographer's dream. But make sure to know your destination's laws before getting your camera out.

In many countries, taking pictures of people is not appreciated for various cultural or religious reasons. It is common courtesy to ask before taking a picture. Even if you don't speak the language, pointing to your camera and then toward the person usually does the trick. Needless to say, if the person declines, you need to respect their wishes. If the person agrees, pay it forward by offering to email their picture to them or—at the very least—showing them their photo on your camera screen. Keep in mind that in some destinations, like Cartagena, people make their money by posing for pictures, or have come to accept a tip for being photographed.

AVOID PHOTOS OF CHILDREN

When it comes to children you should put your camera away, especially if you like to share your pictures on social media. Children are not in a legal position to give consent to have their picture taken or to have it shared publicly. Unfortunately, we live in a world where child abuse is rampant thanks to the internet and it is important to remember that a presumably harmless photo is a violation of a child's privacy.

"IF WE DON'T CONTINUE TO CONTINUE TO INVEST IN AND RESPECT THE PLACES WE LOVE TO TRAVEL TO, THEY WON'T BE HERE FOR MUCH LONGER."

CAITLIN MURRAY

FOUNDER,
PURPOSEFUL NOMAD

HOW YOU CAN SUPPORT WOMEN WHILE TRAVELING

VOLUNTEERING WITH WOMEN

Volunteering with women can be a rewarding experience that connects you to the female experience in other countries. In destinations like India, Guatemala, and Kenya, there are a slew of programs that focus on issues impacting women (see resources). These issues range from reproductive rights, education, and hygiene programs to vocational training and economic security. Look for volunteer opportunities in developing nations such as Sambhali Trust in Jodhpur, which aims to empower local women and children.

SUPPORTING WOMEN AS YOU TRAVEL

Choice and action are critical to feminist travel. Travelers can support local women by making a pledge to shop at women-owned businesses. Whether you're opting to grab a coffee at a female-owned bakery in Brooklyn or to shop for your souvenirs at a women's artisan shop in Guatemala, supporting women in business is the best way to make a difference as you travel.

Beyond visiting women-owned businesses, you can check out the Women Owned initiative, which places Women-Owned logos on consumer products and aims to bring more visibility to female entrepreneurs. They also offer an online directory of women-owned companies to buy from.

MAKING AN EFFORT TO CONNECT WITH LOCAL WOMEN

We are often told that by simply visiting a country we are positively impacting the local economy. However, when participating in tourism that discourages the traveler from leaving their hotel, a myriad of unintended consequences can arise. From the overconsumption of sparse natural resources to steril-

NIKKI VARGAS

Nestled in the small town of San Juan La Laguna, in Guatemala, is a women's cooperative called Casa Flor Ixcaco. This women's weaving group uses 100 percent natural dyes and hand-picked cotton to create devastatingly beautiful clothes, scarves, and bags by hand. Casa Flor Ixcaco both respects the natural process of Mayan weaving while also supporting women in the community. Instead of buying Guatemalan textiles from overpriced stores in main cities or at the airport, I choose to spend my money at Casa Flor Ixcaco and get a high-quality souvenir with a great story.

ized "cultural shows" offered by hotels, your money is better spent looking for meaningful ways to connect with local women.

EDUCATE YOURSELF ON ISSUES FACING WOMEN

Before you travel to any country, learn about its current social and political movements as it impacts local women. We are often granted hot takes of current cultural climates from people who have visited your next destination, but seldom hear the voices of the women who are living there. Over two million blog articles are posted every day, and with a little searching you can find the voices of local women who help round out a more complete picture of the place you are going to and the issues facing women there today. Look specifically for the voices of marginalized communities and learn about the issues that are important to them. This is crucial to helping you have a more meaningful experience as a traveler.

INSPIRE OTHER WOMEN TO TRAVEL

Our authentic stories as female travelers are often overlooked at best and, at worst, repackaged into a clichéd misrepresentation of women traveling today. By writing your blog, sharing your long posts on social media, and telling your friends about your travels, you are declaring your agency and ability to travel freely in the world. Sharing your experience can inspire other women to travel and ensure female travelers appear as they actually are: diverse and independent.

WHAT TO KNOW BEFORE YOU
VOLUNTEER ABROAD

Volunteering abroad not only feels good but can have a positive impact on the world. When selecting a volunteer opportunity there is a lot to consider. It is important that we make sure our best intentions do not harm others in the name of misguided altruism. There are many pitfalls to avoid while traveling, and some volunteer organizations create programs designed to cater to tourists' needs while exploiting locals to turn a profit. When looking for an ethical opportunity that is right for you, there are a few things to keep in mind.

COMMUNITY AND PERSONAL INTEREST ALIGNMENT

When identifying ethical tourism opportunities, visit the organization's website to make sure it is working with local communities on long-term projects that are both needed and wanted by the served community. Sometimes that means you are the resident banana cutter for monkey rehabilitation centers and the elephant poop scooper at others. Being flexible and open to uncomfortable experiences are tools of the volunteering trade.

THE DARK SIDE OF VOLUNTEER TOURISM

Volunteer tourism is a billion-dollar industry that, when abused, looks like unqualified tourists teaching English and posing with children for a few days. A good gauge of intent is to ask would-be volunteers: Would you still be keen to participate if no cameras or pictures were allowed? Is the volunteer planning to use the trip to gain résumé and medical experience while avoiding the red tape of their own country? Navigating the volunteer space in an ethical way requires that we recognize, as travelers and visitors, that these opportunities are labors of love and that being of service to a community is the higher goal.

SUPPORTING CHILDREN

Volunteers that wish to work with children should expect a minimum three-month commitment, bring a specific skill to the organization, and avoid taking jobs away from local businesses or staff. You can also donate to organizations that support families, help alleviate poverty, and increase access to education. If you plan to work with a children's orphanage, make sure that they are accredited and avoid working directly with children in the short term as you may be doing more harm than good. Travelers are often unaware of the damage they may cause when volunteering with children in schools and orphanages without doing their research first.

MEDICAL VOLUNTEERING

When identifying medical volunteer opportunities, keep in mind the treatment of local healthcare professionals and the longevity of the program you are attending. Many programs, like ReSurge International and Smile Train, function not only to serve local communities but to train local healthcare professionals for long-term care as well. Short-term work can be effective if linked to a long-term local partner for checkups and medications. The organization you choose should be culturally literate and fill roles that are needed by the community.

HOW TO AVOID
VOLUNTEER SCAMS

Prospective volunteers have a smorgasbord of opportunities to choose from. While the initial search for the perfect volunteer opportunity can feel a bit overwhelming, here are some ways to avoid scams:

CERTIFICATIONS TO LOOK OUT FOR

Certified B Corporations (B Corps) balance purpose and profit. They are legally required to consider the impact of their decisions on their workers, customers, suppliers, community, and the environment. The ChildSafe Movement provides people with the tools to help keep children safe by providing the highest standard of protection and advice to individuals, businesses, and governmental and non-governmental organizations. Fair Trade Volunteering was created and established by leading volunteer organizations and advisers in the travel industry and helps to ensure volunteer projects benefit both the volunteer and the community.

AVOID ORGANIZATIONS THAT SIDESTEP BACKGROUND CHECKS

If a volunteer organization does not require a background check or some vetting of its applicants, there is a high possibility that the volunteer opportunity is less focused on making a difference and more focused on the tourists' wallet.

KEEP AN EYE OUT FOR UNETHICAL MARKETING

Images of starving children or abused animals used to lure unsuspecting volunteers should be highly suspect. Organizations should treat those they serve with respect and dignity. Parading images of misfortune reduces the subjects to nameless victims.

Children should be protected, not paraded around strangers. Tours that feature schools or orphanages as a stop on the itinerary should be avoided.

BE CAREFUL OF ORGANIZATIONS THAT DON'T REQUIRE CERTIFICATION

If you're keen to teach English but are not being asked about your Test of English as a Foreign Language (TOEFL) certification, that might be a problem. If you're volunteering to provide healthcare in any capacity but aren't asked about medical training or certification, that's a red flag. Bona fide volunteer organizations will care about their applicants having the proper certifications required of the program they are applying for.

KNOW HOW YOUR VOLUNTEER FEES ARE BEING USED

How are tourism dollars being used? If a sanctuary accepts money from visiting tourists, they should be transparent about how they use that funding. While it's not unusual to pay for a volunteer program, most often you'll be informed of where exactly your money is going, such as accommodations and meals for volunteers. Programs that are not transparent with how volunteer fees are being used should be cause for concern.

WHAT TO ASK BEFORE YOU VOLUNTEER

- Is there a rigorous volunteer selection process?

- Does the program include a background check?

- Does the organization offer support for any legal requirements or visas?

- Are there clear expectations of work hours and days?

- What does the training and onboarding schedule look like? (A good rule of thumb is three days of training that include instruction in the local customs and rules.)

- Are you assigned a mentor or contact person to answer questions?

- Is your role as a volunteer in a support position that does not replace the role of a qualified full-time employee?

- Are emergency plans for the organization and the individuals in place?

- Are there regular evaluation meetings for the volunteer?

- Is the organization transparent about the spending of application fees?

VOLUNTEERING
WITH ANIMALS

The travel industry is plagued by unethical animal tourism, but the good news is that tourism companies are now trying to increase education among travelers on what constitutes an ethical animal encounter. TripAdvisor and its booking service, Viator, have removed many animal-based attractions from its site. Instagram now targets photos of animal selfies by showcasing warnings that refer to animal cruelty. Airbnb partnered with PETA to offer vetted animal experiences committed to responsible animal tourism. Travel bloggers are spotlighting ethical animal experiences and, in turn, travelers are now making more informed decisions on responsible wildlife tourism. Fighting unethical animal tourism begins with the traveler. If there is no demand for riding elephants, then those experiences will slowly begin to disappear altogether. Here are some ways you can avoid unethical animal attractions.

KELLY LEWIS

I was at Elephant Nature Park—an elephant sanctuary in Northern Thailand—with founder Lek Chailert. Lek spoke of the plight of the Asian elephant and how she started what seemed like an impossible project at the time. For years, Lek felt great sorrow for elephants that were used for tourism in Southeast Asia. She watched many elephants being separated from their parents and, sometimes, she watched them die. She dreamed of creating a sanctuary where elephants could roam free. During that visit, I happily paid to volunteer with the pachyderms, slinging fruit to elephants with glee, knowing that my dollars were supporting an ethical park.

LOOK FOR ORGANIZATIONS THAT FOCUS ON THE ANIMAL

Riding with elephants? Posing with bears? Cuddling with tigers? These experiences place the emphasis on the traveler as opposed to the well-being of the animals. Elephants don't like to be ridden, bears don't enjoy posing, tigers are not meant to be cuddled—this is a cute way of saying that wild animals are just that: wild! Keep your distance for your own safety and that of the animal. If you are booking an animal experience, you need to be honest with yourself about who this encounter is benefiting—you or the animal. If the answer is not the animal, then chances are this organization is less concerned with animal welfare and more focused on turning a profit.

THINK BEFORE YOU POST

Whether you have twenty or twenty thousand followers, your social media presence has the ability to influence other people. For this reason, it is crucial to be conscious of what you are posting and what animal experiences you are spotlighting. Rather than pay that street vendor in Morocco for a photo with their snake—which is *not* dancing, but rather swaying as a fearful defense to the pipe being played—you are better off spotlighting an ethical animal organization.

REPORT ANIMAL CRUELTY

If you spot any form of animal cruelty during your travels, make sure to report it to the local police, tourism office, or animal welfare society. A simple report can help end the cycle of abuse for an animal living in pain.

HOW TO FIND AN ETHICAL ANIMAL SANCTUARY

Just because an organization uses the word "sanctuary" doesn't necessarily mean it's ethical. Do your research and ask the right questions. Are the animals being made to perform in any way? If animals in a sanctuary are being made to do tricks or entertain tourists, this is not a real sanctuary. What is the animal's backstory? Ethical sanctuaries are emotionally invested in the backstory of their animals and can speak confidently as to how the animals came to the shelter.

LOOK AT WHAT OTHER TRAVELERS ARE SAYING

If you're considering a visit to an animal shelter or sanctuary, take a look at what other travelers have to say about their visit. Well-meaning travelers will take to social media, review sites, or write blogs to share their experiences; if unethical practices were detected, a simple online search will likely reveal it.

LOOK OUT FOR ANIMALS THAT HAVE BEEN MODIFIED

Is that lion missing its teeth? Are those birds' wings broken? Is that tiger declawed? If animals are being modified for tourists' safety, you are *not* at an ethical animal center. When in doubt, check the Global Federation of Animal Sanctuaries (GFAS), a nonprofit organization committed to improving the quality of animal sanctuaries around the globe.

BRINGING HOME
A FUR BABY

When traveling, it can be heartbreaking to see street dogs with swollen bellies and flies in their eyes lying helplessly by the side of the road. Beyond any volunteer program, the best thing you can do for any stray dog or feral cat is to give them a forever home.

KNOW THE THIRTY-DAY RULE

The United States requires a thirty-day waiting period, post-rabies vaccine, before an animal can enter the country. What this means is that if you fall in love with an unvaccinated dog or cat abroad, you are now confronted with three choices: You can get the dog or cat vaccinated in their home country and wait thirty days before traveling, you can get the dog or cat vaccinated in their home country and return thirty days later to pick him or her up, or you can bring the unvaccinated or recently vaccinated dog or cat into the country and have them quarantined at the point of entry. The Centers for Disease Control and Prevention (CDC) outlines the necessary requirements for bringing animals into the United States. Regardless of what you decide, if you are adopting an animal from a high-risk country, there is a mandatory thirty-day waiting period before your fur baby can enter the United States.

CONTACT YOUR AIRLINE IMMEDIATELY

Once you familiarize yourself with the vaccine requirements for your new pet, it is now time to contact your airline. Different airlines have different weight and size restrictions when it comes to flying with animals. If you are bringing home a cat or small puppy, you'll likely be able to bring the animal into the

NIKKI VARGAS

On a trip to Belize, I came across a young puppy with big brown eyes and floppy ears living in the sandy dirt of Caye Caulker—an island off the coast of Belize City. This puppy had been brought to an outdoor shelter where he was living among a family of stray dogs and feral cats under the care of a local man named Kenny. After spending a week visiting the shelter and walking the dogs, my boyfriend and I decided to adopt the pup, who we named Chico, and give him a forever home in New York City.

cabin with you, whereas larger dogs will have to be transported in cargo. If you are traveling with an animal in cargo, many airlines have restrictions around placing animals in the cargo hold if the air outside exceeds or falls below a certain temperature. Call your airline to learn their restrictions as well as any associated fees for traveling with an animal.

GET LOCAL HELP

If adopting a dog or cat abroad, check to see if there is a local Humane Society chapter or other organization that works with assisting foreigners in pet adoption. Beyond the Humane Society, you may be able to connect with locals willing to check in on your puppy during the thirty-day waiting period. If you're adopting an animal from afar, local connections are key.

BRINGING YOUR PET HOME

Your new pet is about to have the trip of a lifetime as it prepares to leave behind its home for the great unknown. As excited as you are, your pet is likely terrified. Calming pet supplies for both cats and dogs—such as collars, pheromone sprays, and CBD-infused treats—are useful for low-stress traveling. These supplies can be purchased from most pet stores and do not require a veterinarian consultation.

NOTE Depending on where you're flying from, the United States will require proof of rabies vaccination upon entry. It can take thirty days from injection before an animal is able to enter the States (or quarantine upon arrival). Check the CDC site for information on animal entry requirements.

FLYING WITH A NEW PET

If you're adopting a dog or cat abroad, you'll need to fly them home. Before you do, here are some suggestions of things to bring and do first.

- Have your pet's rabies certificate and vaccination record printed out.

- Purchase an airline-approved carrier or kennel.

- Call your airline ahead of time to confirm their pet policy.

- Bring a leash, collar, and tags.

- Pack a collapsible water bowl.

- For puppies, bring wee-wee pads for on-the-go bathroom time.

- For cats, bring a collapsible litter box and small sealed bag of litter.

- Consider CBD or a calming collar to alleviate travel anxiety.

- For dogs with separation anxiety, try a Smart Pet Snuggle Puppy.

- Pack snacks and food.

- Bring any medications required for your pet.

- Arrange your on-the-ground transportation ahead of time.

BUILDING
YOUR OWN
FEMINIST
CITY
GUIDE

You've chosen your destination, you've found an affordable flight, you've done your research. Now, it's time to hit the road and build your feminist city guide. To use this section, fill in the blanks and refer to the pages listed for inspiration. When you're done, tear out the pages so you can take the guide with you. Let's get started!

SEE, DO, GO

In this section, brainstorm ideas of where you want to visit once you arrive at your destination. Though you do not have to visit every place you list, it will give you a good idea of what resonates with you.

EAT AND DRINK

Put those research skills to the test! Look for places that go beyond satisfying a craving. Look for eateries that are women-owned, support the LGBTQIA+ community, or employ refugees. A good place to start is the chamber of commerce or women's business associations. (See pages 141–43 for info on how to best support women while you travel.)

1) _____
2) _____
3) _____
4) _____
5) _____

SHOPS AND SPAS

Sometimes a little rest and relaxation are just what we need when traveling. By taking the time to spend money at local and/or woman-owned businesses, you are both bolstering the local economy as well as supporting women. While out and about, if you see women selling goods on the street, pay the full price they ask and offer a tip of a dollar or two if you take their picture.

Strike up a conversation with the owner of a woman-owned business. This is a great way to learn more about their story and to appreciate your time there.

1) _____

2) _____

3) _____

4) _____

5) _____

FEMALE-LED TOURS OR WOMEN-ONLY GROUP TRIPS

One of the quickest ways to get to know a city is to take a day trip, join a multi-day tour, or book a group trip. There are many tour operators that offer women-only group trips or female-led tours to destinations around the globe (see resources). Whether you're interested in booking a women-only walking tour of Paris or a women-only safari in South Africa, look to support a female tour guide or female-owned tour company.

- Tour operator: _____
- Guide name: _____
- Destination: _____
- Meet-up point: _____
- Tour details: _____

PRO TIPS

Be sure to rate and leave positive reviews for women-owned businesses you visit. This helps them gain more customers.

Spotlight women-owned shops or restaurants you love on your social media to help other travelers discover them.

VOLUNTEERING WHILE YOU TRAVEL

Volunteering can be a rewarding experience both at home and abroad. Before you sign up for a volunteer experience, take a look at the "What to Ask Before You Volunteer" checklist (see page 148) and check out our list of volunteer organizations (see resources).

- Organization: _____
- Location: _____
- Dates: _____
- Transportation: _____
- Notes: _____

MUSEUMS AND CULTURAL EXPERIENCES

A quick way to dive deeper into a culture is to visit a museum or book a local experience. Look for museums that explore the lives and experiences of marginalized communities for a more nuanced understanding of a place. Similarly, cultural festivals will offer a richness to your experience that is not to be missed. If looking to connect with locals, search for experiences you can book (see resources).

- Museum: _____
- Hours/days of operation: _____
- Festivals: _____
- Name, date, location, info: _____

- Museum: _____
- Hours/days of operation: _____
- Festivals: _____
- Name, date, location, info: _____

- Museum: _____
- Hours/days of operation: _____
- Festivals: _____
- Name, date, location, info: _____

- Museum: _____
- Hours/days of operation: _____
- Festivals: _____
- Name, date, location, info: _____

PRO TIPS

If you opt for a self-guided audio or walking tour of a city, plan your tour to end before sunset, know where the tour ends, and how you will return to your hotel.

Plan to see attractions that are located in the same area on the same day. See if you can walk or ride a bike in between sights.

ITINERARY

Now that you have ideas about what you want to experience, use the itinerary (see pages 164–165) to block out when you would want to do each activity. This guide can be used either hour by hour or by portion of the day.

	MONDAY	**TUESDAY**	**WEDNESDAY**
MORNING			
AFTERNOON			
EVENING			

THURSDAY	FRIDAY	SATURDAY	SUNDAY

SPACE FOR PLANNING

NOTES:
QUICK REFERENCE

ACCOMMODATIONS

- Hotel address: _____
- Check-in/check-out date: _____
- Check-in/check-out time: _____
- Transportation: _____

FLIGHT INFORMATION

Outbound

- Airline: _____
- Flight number: _____
- Date: _____
- Depart (boarding time): _____
- Arrival (local time and date): _____

Return

- Airline: _____
- Flight number: _____
- Date: _____
- Depart (boarding time): _____
- Arrival (local time and date): _____

BASIC PHRASES TO TRANSLATE

- Hello: _____
- Thank you: _____
- Please: _____
- Yes / No: _____
- How much does this cost?: _____
- Can I take a photo?: _____

ALLERGY GUIDE

- I cannot eat . . . _____
- Nuts _____
  _____
  _____
- Fish _____
  _____
  _____
- Gluten _____
  _____
  _____
- I am a vegetarian _____
  _____
  _____

PRO TIP

If you suffer from allergies, consider purchasing an allergy translation card with images before your trip.

HEALTH AND SAFETY

- Bank address near your hotel:
  _____
  _____
  _____
  _____
  _____

- Travel insurance policy number and contact information:
  _____
  _____
  _____
  _____
  _____

- Embassy contact information:
  _____
  _____
  _____
  _____
  _____

- Tourist police phone number:
  _____
  _____
  _____
  _____
  _____

- Translation of medications and allergies:
  _____
  _____
  _____
  _____
  _____

FEMINIST TRAVEL TREASURE HUNT

Visit or volunteer at a locally based organization that supports women.

Strike up a conversation with a local female business owner.

Celebrate women's historical impact by visiting a local museum or statue.

Pay your respects at the grave of a historical female figure.

Book a local experience, such as a cooking class with a female chef or home cook.

Write a blog or social media post sharing how you supported women on your travels.

Donate to a local nonprofit supporting women in your destination.

Read a book highlighting women or women's history in the destination you are visiting.

Book a female-led walking tour or day trip.

Comment on a blog written by a local female writer.

Meet with a local woman for coffee.

Dine at a woman-owned restaurant during your trip.

Buy an item at a woman-owned store and leave a positive review.

Introduce yourself to another solo female traveler.

On your last day, donate remaining currency to a nonprofit that supports women.

Share this book with a female family member or a friend to inspire their future travels.

Spotlight a woman-owned store or restaurant you love on your social media.

Visit a women's cooperative and learn about the work that they do.

ESSENTIAL TRAVEL RESOURCES

AIRBNB EXPERIENCES

Beyond using Airbnb to book accommodations, you can book anything from cooking classes to walking tours to private concerts via their Experiences portal. This is a great way to connect with locals and learn about the culture.

AIRFORDABLE

Airfordable is a service that allows you to book a flight and pay for it over monthly installments leading up to your departure. Once paid off, you'll receive your boarding pass.

EATWITH

Download EatWith, an app that lets you enjoy dining experiences with locals and other travelers. From arepa parties in a Brooklyn apartment to a Mediterranean-style brunch in Israel, check out the options available in cities around the world.

HAPPYCOW

Find vegan and vegetarian options around the world with HappyCow. The app features more than a hundred thousand coffee shops and restaurants globally with vegan and veggie-friendly options.

HOPPER

Hopper is a useful mobile app that tracks airfare price fluctuations. Download the app and add in your destination and travel dates, and Hopper will alert you when it is the best possible time to book.

PACKPOINT

Drop the stress of packing with PackPoint, an app that checks the weather in advance for you. Input your travel destination and length of trip, and the app will automatically create a packing list for you.

SKIPLAGGED

Skiplagged is another airfare search engine, which specializes in showing you "hidden city" routes to help you find a cheap airfare.

SKYSCANNER

Search for flight deals with Skyscanner's app. If unsure of where to travel next, their "anywhere" search option brings up destinations in order of airfare costs from your location.

TOURLINA

Tourlina is an app that allows female travelers to meet one another while on the road. Plan your tour, plug in your dates, and you'll see a network of women travelers who have an interest in going to the same place at the same time. Users are verified by logging in via their Facebook account.

TRIPIT

Keep track of all of your travel details with TripIt, an app that helps organize your documents in one place. Track your hotel reservations, flight details, and frequent flier miles without ever leaving the app—and send them to whoever might need to know your travel plans too.

TRIPOSO

Download city guides to your phone with Triposo, which aims to replace the need for traditional guidebooks. One of the best features of this app is their offline maps, which don't require a Wi-Fi connection to use. Use Triposo to book hotels, restaurants, and tours as well.

TRIPWHISTLE GLOBAL SOS

TripWhistle helps to ensure your safety by logging your coordinates and calling for help at the push of a button. Using your location information to track where you are, the app shows you the emergency response numbers in the country you're visiting and can dial them too.

WITHLOCALS

Withlocals allows travelers to add in their trip dates and destinations and see a list of experiences offered by locals. The experiences range from medina tours in Marrakech to walking trips through Munich.

WOMEN-ONLY TOUR OPERATORS

INTREPID TRAVEL
Intrepid Travel is a tour company offering a variety of group trips. They offer a line of women-only, female-led tours to countries like Iran, Jordan, and Morocco.

JOURNEYS DISCOVERING AFRICA
Of the many safaris and tours they offer throughout Africa, Journeys Discovering Africa also offers women-only tours in Uganda and South Africa.

ORIGIN TRAVELS
A woman-founded tour company that specializes in women-only adventure retreats to countries like Costa Rica and Kenya.

PURPOSEFUL NOMAD
This female-founded tour company specializes in small group tours designed exclusively for women or families. Purposeful Nomad offers trips to countries like India, Guatemala, and Mongolia with an emphasis on responsible travel.

WOMEN'S ADVENTURE NZ
This female-founded tour group offers women-only activities and multi-day trips throughout New Zealand.

DAMESLY
A woman-owned boutique tour company offering women-only trips with a focus on self-discovery and adventure.

RESOURCES FOR CONNECTING WITH LOCAL WOMEN

FACEBOOK GROUPS FOR SOLO FEMALE TRAVELERS:

• Girls Gone Global

• Girls LOVE Travel

• The Solo Female Traveler Network

• Wanderful

• Women's Travel Community

BUMBLE BFF

Get online and find new female friends on Bumble BFF, the dating website's platonic friend-finding sister site. You could also choose to switch your profile to finding a date, but that's totally up to you. Either way, it's a great way to chat with someone who is local to where you're traveling, and to potentially make a new friend.

COUCHSURFING

CouchSurfing is a website that allows you to stay for free at a host's home (often in their spare room or on their couch). This is a great way of getting to know friendly locals and traveling on a budget. Just do your due diligence and check the reviews before you go. If you feel uncomfortable staying with a male host, request only female hosts or couples.

MEETUP

Check out Meetup to see a host of local events. From surf clubs to poetry performances, this is a great resource for travelers looking to connect with locals.

SERVAS INTERNATIONAL

Servas is a worldwide community of hosts and travelers with a common goal of peace, goodwill, and understanding. Register to be a host, or register as a guest and you'll be connected to a group of like-minded travelers who will host you in their homes. The community currently has over fifteen thousand families and individuals in more than one hundred countries.

TOURSBYLOCALS

Getting into a busy city and just want a little help getting oriented? Hiring a tour guide for the day is a great way to do that. ToursByLocals has a host of tour guides around the world, available for half- and full-day tours.

WORLD WIDE OPPORTUNITIES ON ORGANIC FARMS (WWOOF)

Volunteer to work on a farm at WWOOF—World Wide Opportunities on Organic Farms—where you'll get free room and board in exchange for labor.

RESOURCES FOR TRAVELERS OF COLOR

BLACK & ABROAD

A travel and lifestyle company with a focus on redefining the experiences of travelers of color. Black & Abroad is an excellent resource and offers trips that can be booked via their website.

LATINAS WHO TRAVEL

This bilingual community was created to empower Latina women to travel more. The group connects Latina travelers via events, meet-ups, and group trips.

MUSLIM TRAVEL GIRL

This website is a great online community for millennial Muslim women looking to travel the world on a budget.

NOMADNESS TRAVEL TRIBE

This award-winning lifestyle brand provides resources for urban millennial travelers and encompasses a Facebook community, digital series, and a wide array of group trips.

TASTEMAKERS AFRICA

Tastemakers Africa is a company offering day tours, group trips, and events focused on connecting travelers of color to Africa.

TRAVEL NOIRE

This digital media company provides products and services for millennials from the African diaspora. They offer group trips and online courses designed to empower and educate Black travelers.

RESOURCES FOR LGBTQIA+ TRAVELERS

DIVA DESTINATIONS

Diva Destinations is a UK-based lesbian tour operator that hosts lesbian group holidays around Europe. They offer an annual group trip to the Eressos International Women's Festival in Greece, as well as river cruises around Europe. There are trips that cater to couples as well as trips for solo travelers, and the Diva Destinations tours are not limited to travelers from the UK.

INTERNATIONAL LESBIAN, GAY, BISEXUAL, TRANS, AND INTERSEX ASSOCIATION

Both the ILGA (International Lesbian, Gay, Bisexual, Trans, and Intersex Association) and the IGLTA (International LGBTQIA+ Travel Association) have comprehensive resources for queer travelers on their websites. The ILGA offers a detailed overview of sexual orientation laws around the world, while the ILGTA has good trip-planning tools for LGBTQIA+ travelers.

OLIVIA TRAVEL

Olivia is the largest lesbian travel company offering all-lesbian vacations ranging from cruises and adventure trips to resorts. Olivia always buys out a whole resort or charters the entire ship to make sure the trip is a safe space for lesbian women.

PURPLE ROOFS

Purple Roofs is the largest travel directory for LGBTQIA+ friendly accommodations. Purple Roofs is a great resource for lesbian-owned and lesbian-friendly hotels, B&Bs, and vacation rentals, listing over 4,800 properties around the world. TAG Approved hotels, which are hotels that are not only LGBTQIA+ friendly but also support the LGBTQIA+ community in their employment policies and services, are also recommended. There are around 2,000 TAG Approved hotels.

R FAMILY VACATIONS

R Family Vacations was founded by Rosie O'Donnell, and what was once limited to LGBTQIA+ family cruises has now grown into other kinds of LGBTQIA+ family vacations. R Family Vacations has also launched an "adult vacation" line for kid-free getaways.

VOLUNTEER RESOURCES

ANGKOR HOSPITAL FOR CHILDREN

Founded in 1999 with the goal of becoming a world-class hospital for Cambodians, this hospital accepts medical volunteers trained in pediatric medicine or pediatric subspecialties.

ANIMAL EXPERIENCE INTERNATIONAL

A certified B Corp offering animal-related volunteer opportunities at sanctuaries, hospitals, and animal-focused research projects.

ANJALI HOUSE

This locally run organization in Cambodia supports one hundred and twenty youths, ages five to ten, to break the cycle of poverty. Anjali House accepts twenty volunteers each year for programs focused on education, arts, and health care.

A BROADER VIEW VOLUNTEERS

This US-based nonprofit offers an array of vetted social and conservation projects across multiple countries. Programs last anywhere from one to twelve weeks.

ELEPHANT NATURE PARK
Elephant Nature Park is a female-founded sanctuary in Northern Thailand that cares for rescued elephants, dogs, and cats. Volunteers can come for a day visit, stay overnight, or volunteer long term to help care for and feed the animals.

GLOBAL FEDERATION OF ANIMAL SANCTUARIES
The Global Federation of Animal Sanctuaries (GFAS) is a nonprofit organization committed to improving the quality of animal sanctuaries around the globe. The GFAS website offers a nifty online search tool that allows travelers to search for vetted and GFAS accredited animal sanctuaries.

ONE SKY FOUNDATION
One Sky Foundation works closely with children and their families in Thailand to foster independence and avoid institutions. Short-term volunteers will be considered only if they can bring a much-needed skill that is not available locally.

SAMBHALI TRUST
An NGO based in Jodhpur, Sambhali Trust works to empower marginalized women experiencing discrimination and violence due to economic, gender, and/or caste status.

ACKNOWLEDGMENTS

We want to take a moment to offer our complete gratitude to the many friends, family, and readers who have supported *Unearth Women* on its journey. What began as nothing more than a wild idea back in 2018 has blossomed into an international print and digital magazine, a community of supportive women, and a book that speaks to the nuanced experience of women's travel. Launching a new publication comes with its fair share of trials, yet *Unearth Women* continues to blossom because of the countless people who have shared their voices, stories, and talents with our platform and continue to support our work. It is the greatest privilege to both celebrate the accomplishments of women and to inspire readers to see the world in a new, more mindful way.

There are many people who were instrumental in the process of writing this book. First, we want to thank our editor, Gabrielle Van Tassel, and the entire Clarkson Potter team for bringing this book to life. We were originally approached by Gabrielle with the idea for this book and cannot thank her enough for taking a chance on *Unearth Women*. Her guidance and editing were instrumental in bringing this book to life. We also want to thank Lucy Engelman, whose beautiful illustrations pepper the pages of this text.

Of course, this book would not exist without the help of our talented contributors who shared their expertise and experiences. Each chapter combines the voices of Oneika Raymond, Brooke Saward, Dani Heinrich, Annika Ziehen, Kelly Lewis, and Esme Benjamin. Thank you to Oneika, whose packing expertise and advice for travelers of color proved instrumental to this book. Thank you to Brooke, whose experiences as a solo traveler helped single-handedly shape chapter 5. Thank you to Dani, who speaks candidly about her experiences traveling as a lesbian today and offers resources for other LGBTQIA+ travelers. Thank you to Annika, whose insatiable appetite for adventure and useful travel tips are key to trip planning. Thank you to Kelly, who tackles such crucial topics as responsible travel and dealing with your period abroad. And, finally, thanks to Esme who offers her expertise in all things wellness.

To our investor, Stacey Empson, we want to say thank you for your unyielding belief in *Unearth Women*. We are forever grateful for your support in helping to turn the idea of a women's travel magazine into an internationally sold reality. And to our loved ones who have supported us in more ways than one, there are not enough words to express our gratitude.

FROM NIKKI: Thank you to Jeff Cerulli, who infuses my life with an endless supply of love, happiness, laughter, and joy. You are my best friend and champion. I love you more than words can say. Thank you to the Cerulli family for their love, kindness, and generosity. Thank you to my own parents, Axel Vargas, Yana Nedvetsky, Karen Hull, and Chris Bertelsen, who have brought me up with the unwavering ambition to chase my dreams, no matter how far-fetched they may seem. Thank you for your love, your support, and the boundless opportunities in life you have granted me. Thank you to my sister and brother, Natalie Vargas-Nedvetsky and Jan Vargas-Nedvetsky, who continue to inspire me every day as they blossom in their own creative endeavors. Thank you to my dearly departed grandmother, Amparo Abad, whose laugh I can still hear and smile I can still see clearly. Thank you to my other grandmother, Clarita Herrera, whose passion for life and unquenchable thirst for experiences always inspire me. Thank you to my dear friends Esme Benjamin, Amber Snider, and Rachel Gould, who have been there for me through thick and thin. You three are my rock and I am grateful to have you in my life. Last but not least, thank you to my friend and business partner, Elise Fitzsimmons. I am endlessly thankful to be on this adventure with you, to survive the lows and celebrate the highs together, and to grow stronger as friends because of it. Thank you for believing in me and this publication.

FROM ELISE: Thank you to my parents, Pat and Shelley Fitzsimmons, my anchors in the most turbulent of storms and advocates for every half- (and full-) brained idea I have had thus far. To my brothers, Charles and Will, and their partners, thank you for the constant supply of laughter and wisdom. Your intellect asks me to think harder about my "why." Thank you to my family—from New York to Sacramento and countless cities in between—the dozens of you who are a soft place to land in questionable terrain and standard-bearers for full, connected lives. Special thanks to the women in my family—each a pioneer in her own right, demonstrating what is possible and attainable for women. Not only living examples of what can be accomplished on their own terms, these women showed me how to act in service, strength, and love. To the tribes of friends spanning time zones and beliefs, thank you for inspiring me to hike the extra mile, laugh harder, love deeper, fully commit, and send it. Last, but always first in my heart, thank you, Nikki Vargas. My oldest friend and partner in manifesting goals, your tenacity helped me believe in the power of possibility—that the spark of an idea is all you need to have a movement catch fire.

ABOUT THE CONTRIBUTORS

ANNIKA ZIEHEN is a travel writer and published author from Germany. After having lived in New York and Cape Town for many years, she now travels the world as a digital nomad and writes about her adventures on her blog, *The Midnight Blue Elephant*. She describes herself as a very hungry scuba diver who travels in the pursuit of Nemo, noodles, and champagne. Her trips take her anywhere with an ocean to dive into or a plate of pasta to devour. As an avid solo traveler, Annika has published a book on solo travel and inspires other women to step out into the world by themselves.

BROOKE SAWARD is an author and travel expert. Having visited more than eighty countries, Brooke shares her travel stories, anecdotes, and expertise on her popular blog, *World of Wanderlust*, and in her eponymous book.

DANI HEINRICH is the co-founder of Globe-trotter Girls, an independent travel website on which she shares personal travel stories, practical tips, and LGBTQIA+ experiences. Originally from Germany, Dani became nomadic in 2010, when she quit her desk job in London. Instead of returning to her corporate career, she became a full-time travel blogger, having visited more than sixty countries on five continents.

ESME BENJAMIN is a freelance journalist and host of the travel podcast *The Trip That Changed Me*. She has contributed stories to a slew of publications, from Refinery29 to *SELF*, and in 2019 was the recipient of a MUSE Creative Award in the travel and tourism category. Previously, Esme was an editor at Culture Trip, where she started and developed the wellness vertical, exploring the healing traditions, rituals, and trends of cultures from all over the world. Esme lives in Brooklyn with her husband, Sid, and their corgi, Loaf.

KELLY LEWIS is on the founding team of *Unearth Women* and is a women's travel industry maven, passionate about helping women connect to their personal power through travel. She's the founder of Go! Girl Guides, which publishes the world's first series of travel guidebooks for women, as well as the annual Women's Travel Fest and Damesly, a boutique women's tour company. She's also the author of *Tell Her She Can't*, a book that helps women transform negativity into fuel.

ONEIKA RAYMOND is an award-winning travel and lifestyle expert, journalist, and television host whose adventures have taken her to more than 115 countries on 6 continents. As an NBC New York correspondent and host of two series on the Travel Channel, she's dedicated to inspiring women and people of color to live their best lives both at home and abroad. Profiled by outlets such as *Forbes*, the *Washington Post*, and *New York* magazine, Oneika has written for a wide range of publications, including *Condé Nast Traveler*, *Ebony*, and *Marriott Bonvoy Traveler*. She's also the voice behind the highly respected travel blog *Oneika the Traveller*, which won Best Travel Blog from the Society of American Travel Writers' 2018 Lowell Thomas Awards. She lives in New York City with her husband and daughter.

ABOUT THE

NIKKI VARGAS

Nikki Vargas is a travel editor, journalist, producer, public speaker, and an author based in New York City. She is originally from Bogotá, Colombia. Nikki is the founding editor and co-founder of *Unearth Women*. In addition to her work with *Unearth Women*, Nikki is an editor for Fodor's Travel and previously was a travel editor for *The Infatuation, Atlas Obscura,* and *Culture Trip.* As a journalist, she has had her bylines appear in *Zagat, VICE, Food & Wine, Roads & Kingdoms, Cosmopolitan,* and more.

As a public speaker, Nikki has spoken at various conferences, including the Women's Travel Fest, Women in Travel Summit, Latino Travel Fest, and the *New York Times* Travel Show. In addition, she has produced various video series—from *Culture Trip*'s Hungerlust to *Unearth Women*'s #WomenOwned. Currently, Nikki is a producer for an upcoming documentary made in partnership with Unrealistic Ideas and One Foot Forward.

AUTHORS

ELISE FITZSIMMONS

As *Unearth Women*'s co-founder, Elise Fitzsimmons cares deeply about the representation of women around the world. Elise and her work with *Unearth Women* have been featured in *Travel + Leisure*, the *Washington Post*, *Good Morning America*, Cheddar TV, and more. Elise lives semi-nomadically. When she is not practicing yoga, editing podcasts, or learning about deep space, she can most often be spotted arm-in-arm with new friends discovering hole-in-the-wall eateries.

Use the information in this book as your guide, but always do your research and be mindful of your surroundings when traveling.

Published in the United States by Clarkson Potter/Publishers, an imprint of Random House, a division of Penguin Random House LLC, New York.
clarksonpotter.com

CLARKSON POTTER is a trademark and POTTER with colophon is a registered trademark of Penguin Random House LLC.

Library of Congress Cataloging-in-Publication Data
Names: Vargas, Nikki, author. | Fitzsimmons, Elise, author. | Engelman, Lucy, illustrator.
Title: Wanderess : the unearth women guide to traveling smart, safe, and solo / Nikki Vargas and Elise Fitzsimmons with Brooke Saward, Oneika Raymond, Kelly Lewis, Annika Ziehen, Dani Heinrich, and Esme Benjamin ; illustrations by Lucy Engelman.
Description: New York : Clarkson Potter/Publishers, 2022. Identifiers: LCCN 2021001262 (print) | LCCN 2021001263 (ebook) | ISBN 9780593138496 (paperback) | ISBN 9780593138502 (ebook).
Subjects: LCSH: Women—Travel. | Women travelers. Classification: LCC G156.5.W66 V37 2022 (print) | LCC G156.5.W66 (ebook) | DDC 910.82—dc23. LC record available at https://lccn.loc.gov/2021001262 LC ebook record available at https://lccn.loc.gov/2021001263

ISBN 978-0-593-13849-6
Ebook ISBN 978-0-593-13850-2

Printed in China

Editor: Gabrielle Van Tassel
Designer: Jen Wang
Illustrations: Lucy Engelman
Production Editor: Patricia Shaw
Production Manager: Jessica Heim
Compositors: Merri Ann Morrell and Nick Patton
Copy Editor: Sasha Tropp

10 9 8 7 6 5 4 3 2 1

First Edition